T0337707

# UNSTUDIO

## FALK JAEGER

Fotografien von
Photographs by
Christian Richters

JOVIS

# PORTFOLIO

# UNSTUDIO

## FALK JAEGER

Fotografien von
Photographs by
Christian Richters

JOVIS

Alle vorgestellten Projekte mit Ausnahme privater Wohnhäuser sind mit Koordinaten versehen, die es erlauben, die Standorte der Gebäude z.B. über GoogleEarth exakt zu lokalisieren. For all projects presented with the exception of private housings, coordinates are provided allowing the exact localisation of the buildings via GoogleEarth or other applications.
© 2009 by jovis Verlag GmbH. Das Copyright für die Texte liegt beim Autor. Das Copyright für die Abbildungen liegt bei Christian Richters außer S. 94–97: Jan Derwig, S. 132r., 133: Roland Borgmann und S. 16r. Michael Moran Texts by kind permission of the author. Pictures by kind permission of Christian Richters except p. 94–97: Jan Derwig, p. 132r., 133: Roland Borgmann and p. 16r. Michael Moran I Alle Rechte vorbehalten. All rights reserved. I Die Gesamtreihe Portfolio wird herausgegeben von Falk Jaeger. The series Portfolio is edited by Falk Jaeger. I Umschlagfoto Cover: vorn front Forschungslabor, Groningen Research Laboratory, Groningen, hinten back VilLA NM, upstate New York, Christian Richters I Redaktionelle Mitarbeit Co-editing: Machteld Kors, Karen Murphy, UNStudio I Übersetzung Translation: Rachel Hill, Berlin I Gestaltung und Satz Design and setting: Susanne Rösler, Berlin I Lithografie Lithography: Bild1Druck, Berlin I Druck und Bindung Printing and binding: GCC Grafisches Centrum Cuno, Calbe I Bibliografische Information der Deutschen Bibliothek I Die Deutsche Bibliothek verzeichnet diese Publikation in der Deutschen Nationalbibliografie; detaillierte bibliografische Daten sind im Internet über http://dnb.ddb.de abrufbar. Bibliographic information published by Die Deutsche Bibliothek I Die Deutsche Bibliothek lists this publication in the Deutsche Nationalbibliografie; detailed bibliographic data are available on the Internet at http://dnb.ddb.de
jovis Verlag GmbH I Kurfürstenstraße 15/16 I 10785 Berlin I www.jovis.de I ISBN 978-3-939633-84-6

# INHALT
# CONTENTS

# VORWORT
# FOREWORD

Mit dem Mercedes-Benz Museum in Stuttgart veränderte sich die öffentliche Wahrnehmung des Amsterdamer Architekturbüros UNStudio deutlich. Das junge und frische Avantgardeteam wird nun als international erfolgreich agierendes Architekturbüro gesehen. Zuvor hatte Ben van Berkel bereits in Fachkreisen einen hohen Bekanntheitsgrad erlangt. An den renommierten Hochschulen der Welt als Vortragender und Lehrer, mit Präsentationen auf Symposien sowie mit spektakulären Wettbewerbsbeiträgen war er in der Fachwelt präsent und stellte gemeinsam mit seiner Partnerin Caroline Bos die Beherrschung der publizistischen Klaviatur unter Beweis. Doch anders als die eine Generation ältere Riege der Stararchitekten gelang es ihm frühzeitig, ein leistungsfähiges Team zu bilden, das sich in der Praxis des Architekturbetriebs durchsetzte und dafür sorgte, dass nicht nur Architektur in attraktiven Plänen und hinreißenden Bildern produziert, sondern dass auch gebaut wurde.

Ben van Berkel gehört zu den Architekten, die man auch als Baukünstler bezeichnen möchte, denn seine Architektur ist mehr als die anderer formal gedacht und ausgeprägt. Die Lust am Ausleben formaler Vorstellungen führt wohl auch dazu, dass er sich ebenso gern auf dem Feld des Produktdesigns tummelt. In den Überschneidungen und Verbindungen zwischen Design und Architektur bei Ben van Berkel wird die Verwandtschaft der beiden Gebiete deutlich, die sich bei anderen Architekten zuweilen auch als Hassliebe äußert, wie oft bei nahen Verwandten.

Die Besonderheit von van Berkels Vorgehen liegt darin, dass er in vordergründig architekturfernen Bereichen auf Motivsuche geht, in der Mathematik, der Geometrie, der Kybernetik, und zu Organisationsmodellen kommt, die sich in explizit formale Vorgaben wandeln (Möbiusband, Doppelhelix u. a.). Es mag überraschen, wenn

Public perception of UNStudio architects from Amsterdam changed after they built the Mercedes-Benz Museum in Stuttgart. The young, dynamic avant-garde team has since become an international success. Ben van Berkel was well respected in professional circles beforehand. He was known as a lecturer and teacher at the world's most renowned schools; from presentations at symposia and spectacular contributions to competitions and in collaboration with his partner Caroline Bos, for their joint mastery of the written word. However, in contrast to the older generation of star architects before him, he managed to establish a capable team around him, which has asserted itself in the practical world of architecture. His team not only produces architecture in attractive plans and images, it also manages to have it built.

Ben van Berkel is one of those architects who could be described as a "structural artist"; his architecture is more formally developed and pronounced than that of other architects. The pleasure that he finds in transforming his ideas into reality has led him to also try his hand at product design. Intersections and connections between design and architecture in Ben van Berkel's work expose the relationship between the two; an area that seems to provoke familial love-hate tension in the work of other architects.

The special thing about van Berkel's approach is that he usually finds his motifs in areas which have nothing to do with architecture—mathematics, geometry, cybernetics—leading him to models of organisation that are defined by explicitly formal parameters (Möbius band, double helix, etc.). It is often surprising when in the actual design and implementation phases, formal and spatial structures emerge that are also functional. In producing such functional diagrams his work does not adhere to the rules of "orthodox architecture" (analogous to the term "orthodox medicine").

dann in der konkreten Entwurfsphase und schließlich in der Realisierung aus diesen Entwurfsmodellen nicht nur formale und räumliche Strukturen erwachsen, sondern auch funktionale, denn es entspricht keineswegs den Regeln der „Schularchitektur" (um hier einmal ein Analogon der „Schulmedizin" anzuwenden), auf diese Weise zu Funktionsdiagrammen zu kommen.

Diagrammatische Arbeitsweise ist auch eine vom UNStudio entwickelte Methode, die heutige Komplexität der Informationen, Erkenntnisse und Vorgaben in einen Planungsprozess einzubringen. Es eröffnet sich dadurch die Möglichkeit, schneller und präziser auf komplexe Situationen, bestehend aus städtebaulichen, wirtschaftlichen, soziologischen, psychologischen, also materiellen wie virtuellen Komponenten, zu reagieren. Aus diesem Bewusstsein heraus stellt Ben van Berkel die strengen Dogmen des Modernismus in Frage und setzt dessen durchaus lustfeindlichen Paradigmen der Reduktion und Minimierung (die als Verarmung empfunden werden können) die Verheißung des Reichtums, des Aufblühens entgegen. Architektur soll wieder Lust machen.

Entsprechend den neuen vielschichtigeren Arbeitsweisen haben sich die Strukturen des Büros van Berkel en Bos gewandelt. Den Architekten wurden Experten aus allen denkbaren Fachgebieten zur Seite gestellt. Caroline Bos, die sich nicht als Architektin versteht, ist in diesen Strukturen zu Hause, organisiert und steuert sie. Die Personalisierung war nicht mehr als zeitgemäß empfunden worden, und so war eine Umbenennung des Büros geboten. United Networks für Städtebau, Infrastruktur und Architektur, kurz UNStudio, lautet seit 1998 der Name für das multinationale, interdisziplinäre, multipel vernetzte Büro. Somit fühlt man sich für die neuen Herausforderungen an den Berufsstand der Architekten gewappnet.

Diagrammatic working methods have been developed by UNStudio to incorporate today's complexity of information, knowledge and specifications into the planning process. It facilitates quicker and more precise reaction to complex situations comprising urban, economic, sociological and psychological components; the material and the virtual. Ben van Berkel thereby questions the severe dogmas of modernism, counteracting its anti-pleasure paradigms of reduction and minimisation (which could be felt to be of negative effect) with the promise of opulence, of florescence; architecture to whet the appetite.

In correspondence to its new multifaceted working methods, the structure of the van Berkel en Bos office has also changed. The architects are surrounded by experts in all sorts of subject areas. Caroline Bos, who does not consider herself an architect, organises and guides them. It no longer seemed accurate for the name of the office be so personalised and the decision was made to rename it. Since 1998, this multinational, interdisciplinary, multiply networked practice has been known as United Networks for Urban Planning, Infrastructure and Architecture, in short UNStudio, leaving it well equipped for the new challenges that now face the architectural profession.

# VOM DIAGRAMM ZUR FORM ZUM BAUWERK
## FROM DIAGRAM TO FORM TO BUILDING

Die Erfahrungen im weltläufigen London und speziell das Studium an der Architectural Association, einem Fokus der Architekturavantgarde, sind für viele erfolgreiche Architekten Initialzündung einer internationalen Karriere gewesen. Auch für Ben van Berkel und Caroline Bos begann die berufliche und private Zukunftsplanung in London. Er saugte in der Szene alle Ideen in sich auf, sie erwarb durch das Kunstgeschichtsstudium das Rüstzeug für die verbale Kommunikation dessen, was sich im Kopf eines Künstlers und Architekten abspielt, was er denkt, plant und schließlich realisiert.

Die Symbiose der beiden erwies sich als äußerst fruchtbar. Sie entwickelten Ideen, Positionen und Theorien und brachten sie unter die Leute, in Tageszeitungen und Fachblättern, durch Bücher und Ausstellungen. Folgerichtig kam es zu ersten Arbeiten in jener Transferzone zwischen Publizistik und konkretem Bauen, dem Ausstellungswesen. Ben van Berkel entwarf Galerieräume sowie Ausstellungsdesign und das Team van Berkel en Bos steigerte seinen Bekanntheitsgrad kontinuierlich.

Innenarchitektur und drei Bauten in Amersfoort, die Umspannstation (1989–94), der Umbau der Villa Härtel und das Karbouw-Gebäude (beide 1990–92) (▶94) waren die ersten realisierten Projekte. Dass dann keine Ausstellung, auch kein Haus, sondern das Angebot zum Bau eines Ingenieurbauwerks, einer ausgewachsenen Brücke, den Durchbruch brachte, gehört zu den Unwägbarkeiten, aber auch Glücksfällen im Leben, die man jedoch erst einmal ergreifen muss. Die Arbeit an der Erasmusbrücke in Rotterdam (1990–96) (▶60) brachte dem Büro van Berkel en Bos für einige Jahre Substanz und Kontinuität.

Die Kenntnisse, die sich Ben van Berkel angeeignet hat, beschränken sich nicht auf die Historie des Bauens und die Tendenzen der Gegenwartsarchitektur. Ihn bewegen Philosophie und Literatur, Musik und Kunst ebenso, und selbst die verschiedensten Naturwissenschaften sind vor seiner Entdeckerlust nicht sicher. Es ist wohl diese prinzipielle Offenheit und die respektvolle Grundhaltung unterschiedlichsten Ideenwelten gegenüber, die ihn selbst vor einer ideologischen Position gefeit sein lassen. Missionarischer Eifer ist seine Sache nicht. Architektonische Weltentwürfe und Heilslehren, wie sie sonst aus Holland kommen, hat er nicht im Angebot.

Anfang der neunziger Jahre suchte van Berkel nach einem Instrument, die Gleichzeitigkeit der im Raum anzutreffenden Ereignisse, Bedingungen und Aktivitäten als Entwurfsvariablen begrifflich und gedanklich zu fassen. Er fand es in den „Kreuzungspunkten", die sich durch die erkannten Beziehungen ergeben, die allerdings noch keine formbildenden Vorgaben darstellen.

„Mobile Kräfte" ist ein anderer vielbemühter Topos im frühen Werk van Berkels. Obgleich er sich der aus philosophischer Warte in die architekturtheoretische Diskussion eingebrachten Vision von einer fortschreitenden Immaterialisierung und Virtualisierung der Architektur, die durch wachsende Präsenz der Medien und zunehmende Geschwindigkeit aller Lebensumstände bedingt sei, widersetzt, sieht er die Notwendigkeit, den Dynamismus der Gegenwart in der Architektur zum Ausdruck zu bringen.

Erste Anzeichen für diesen gebauten Dynamismus zeigten sich schon bei der Villa Härtel, beim Umspannwerk und beim Karbouw-Haus in Amersfoort, deren Baukörper in Bewegung gebracht wurden. Ein Schlüsselprojekt des Einflusses der „mobilen Kräfte" ist der nicht realisierte Bau für die Firmen Crea & Activa in Nijkerk (1992). Der Baukörper, aus

Experience in the cosmopolitan city of London, and in particular studies at the Architectural Association —a focal point of the avant-garde of architecture— has ignited the international careers of many successful architects. Ben van Berkel and Caroline Bos also began to plan their personal and professional futures in London. He soaked up the ideas floating around in the architectural scene while she through her studies of Art History acquired the skills needed to verbally communicate the thoughts that go through an artist's and architect's mind; what he plans and ultimately builds.

The symbiosis of the two proved extremely fruitful. They developed ideas, positions, and theories, giving people access to them through daily newspapers, professional journals, books, and exhibitions. This led to their first commissions in the intersection between publishing and building: exhibition design. Ben van Berkel designed gallery spaces and exhibitions. The van Berkel en Bos practice became increasingly famous.

Interior architecture and three buildings in Amersfoort—the transformer station (1989–94), the conversion of the Villa Härtel (1990–92), and the Karbouw Building (1990–92) (▶94)—were the first to be erected. However, van Berkel en Bos' breakthrough did not come with an exhibition or a building. As luck and the unpredictability of life would have it, it was the opportunity to realise a civil engineering project—to erect a bridge—that they grasped and which led to their success. Work on the Erasmus Bridge in Rotterdam (1990–96) (▶60) brought continuity and substance to the van Berkel en Bos practice over a period of a few years.

The knowledge that Ben van Berkel has attained is not limited to the history of construction nor to contemporary architectural tendencies. He is interested in philosophy and literature, music and art just as much as science. His basic openness and respectful attitude towards the most diverse worlds of ideas grant him immunity from getting stuck in one ideological position. Missionary zeal is not his thing. He does not offer architectural-world-concepts nor doctrines of salvation as have been known to originate from Holland.

In the early nineties, van Berkel went in search of an instrument that would grasp the events, conditions and activities that co-exist in space from conceptual and theoretical points of view. He found it at the "crossroads" that emerge from familiar associations, but had not yet found spatial form.

"Mobile forces" is another area that was pursued with much effort in the early work of van Berkel. Although he rejects the vision, which has been taken from the field of philosophy into architectural theoretical debate, of a progressive dematerialisation and virtualisation of architecture, caused by a growing media presence and the increasing speed of everyday life, he does feel it necessary to express the dynamism of the present through architecture.

The first signs of this built dynamism are to be seen in Villa Härtel, the transformer station and the Karbouw Building in Amersfoort, whose volumes seem to have been set in motion. A key unbuilt mobile forces project is a building for the Crea & Activa company in Nijkerk (1992). The volume, which was generated from segments of spherical shells, appears to have been shaped by movable forces; it reacts to the sequential perception of car drivers on a neighbouring motorway bridge. Façades and roof surfaces merge as several sides always remain si-

Kugelschalenabschnitten generiert, scheint durch bewegliche Kräfte geformt und reagiert auf die sequenzielle Wahrnehmung durch die Autofahrer auf dem benachbarten Autobahndamm. Fassaden und Dachfläche gehen ineinander über, man kann immer *mehrere* Seiten gleichzeitig sehen. Der Bau präsentiert als Raum-Zeit-Architektur das Ungleichzeitige auf einen Blick (aus dem Seitenfenster).

*Mobile forces* sind auch im österreichischen Innsbruck am Werk. Eine Umspannstation sitzt wie eine arbeitende Maschine im Blockinnenraum eines innerstädtischen Quartiers. Man spürt den Strom vibrieren. Sie ist kein Haus, eher eine Mobilie, die den

den und Fenster. Die karge Materialpalette – Sichtbeton, Natursteinplatten, grauer Schotter, ein wenig honigfarbenes Holz, ein Baumrain, keine Bodendeckerpflanzen – versetzt den Betrachter in südliche Gefilde, falls das Wetter mitspielt.

Die Villa ist in einer Phase entstanden, in der Ben van Berkel sich mit *blob* und *box* auseinandersetzte, der box aber noch den Vorzug gab. Eine Phase, die bis zu den 2001 vollendeten Wasservillen in Almere reicht und in der er keine erkennbaren formalen Eigenheiten entwickelte. Die Praxis, jede Bauaufgabe konzeptionell und gestalterisch neu und unvoreingenommen anzugehen, hat er ohnehin bis heute beibe-

VILLA HÄRTEL, AMERSFOORT (NL) VILLA HÄRTEL, AMERSFOORT (NL) UMSPANNSTATION, AMERSFOORT (NL) TRANSFORMER STATION, AMERSFOORT (NL)
UMSPANNSTATION, INSBRUCK (A), ANSICHT VON WESTEN TRANSFORMER STATION, INSBRUCK (A), VIEW FROM WEST

Eindruck erweckt, man könne sie jederzeit wegfahren. Ihre „Karosserie" mit Stromlinienformen, Kühlerfront und Ladeluke ist aufgebockt. Doch was sich wie eine Metallhaut ausnimmt, ist dunkel-anthrazit schimmernder Lavabasalt, ein Baumaterial für Tempel, und als einen solchen sehen die Architekten die Elektrizitätsstation.

Ein Kontrastprogramm ist die 1992–94 gebaute Villa Wilbrink in Amersfoort, die von der Straße aus nicht gesehen werden will. Ohne Höhensprung steigt das Straßenniveau in Form einer Schotterfläche langsam an und bildet das Dach des Hauses. Erst im rückwärtigen Teil des Grundstücks zeigt es Fassa-

halten. So ist die Kapelle in Hilversum (1995–2000) von der Idee der stereometrischen Box geprägt, die ihre spirituelle Anmutung einzig durch die Lichtführung erfährt. Dabei erlaubt er sich keinerlei Rückgriff auf mit dem Begriff „Kirche" verbundene Erfahrungen und Sehgewohnheiten. Die zur selben Zeit entstandene Müllentsorgungsstation in Delft hingegen entwickelt erheblich Dynamik und durchaus eine gewisse Schönheit aus ihrer morphologischen Genese, die zu einem äußerst signifikanten, wiedererkennbaren Bauwerk führt. Warum sollte eine Müllstation nicht auch schön sein dürfen? Entscheidend für die Angemessenheit ist die Anmutung, denn Ele-

multaneously visible. The building presents the non-simultaneous as space-time-architecture at a glance (out of the side window).

Mobile forces are also at work in the city of Innsbruck, Austria. A Substation sits like a machine inside the block of an inner-city district. You can feel the vibrations of the electricity. It is a movable rather than a building, giving the impression that it could be taken away anytime. Its bodywork with streamlined shapes, a grille front, and loading hatch have been elevated. However, what appears to be a metal skin is actually natural stone, dark anthracite gleaming basalt, a material for a temple, which is

The villa was built during a phase in which Ben van Berkel dealt with both blob and box but still gave preference to the box. It included the water villas in Almere (2001), where the architect did not develop any formally recognisable mannerisms. He has retained the habit to this day of approaching each building task anew and open-mindedly as far as concept and creativity are concerned. The chapel in Hilversum (1995–2000) is therefore based on the idea of a solid geometric box, whose spiritual atmosphere is created by lighting alone. Van Berkel did not fall back on the usual experiences and visual features associated with the term, "church." In

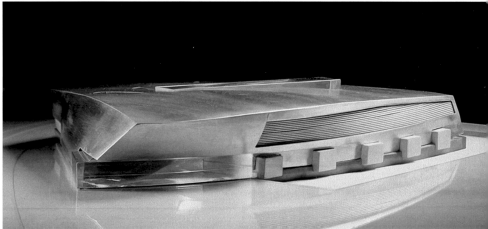

UMSPANNSTATION, INSBRUCK (A), ANSICHT VON NORDOSTEN TRANSFORMER STATION, INSBRUCK (A), VIEW FROM NORTH EAST CREA & ACTIVA, NIJKERK (NL), MODELL CREA & ACTIVA, NIJKERK (NL), MODEL

what the architects consider this transformer station to be.

The Villa Wilbrink in Amersfoort, built in 1992–94, which does not wish to be seen from the street, stands in stark contrast to that. The street level rises gradually as a gravel plane, without a sudden shift in height, to form the roof of the building. Its façades and windows are only visible from the rear of the site. The austere palette of materials—fairfaced concrete, slabs of natural stone, gravel, a little honey-coloured wood, a rough group of trees and a lack of shrubs—transports the observer to southern regions as long as the weather cooperates.

contrast, the waste disposal facility, built in Delft at the same time, demonstrates considerable dynamics and indeed a certain beauty in its morphological genesis, making it a clearly recognisable building. Why shouldn't a waste disposal facility be beautiful? The first impression a building makes defines its appropriateness; elegance, refinement, or expensive surfaces would not have suited this building.

Ijsselstein town hall and theatre, also inaugurated in 2000, is stringently stereometric; oriented towards Mies van der Rohe rather than Le Corbusier. It pragmatically fulfils its function with industrial glass walls—just like the chapel—industrial façades

ganz, Raffinesse oder kostbare Oberflächen wären der Bauaufgabe nicht adäquat.

Wiederum streng stereometrisch, eher an Ludwig Mies van der Rohe denn an Le Corbusier orientiert, das ebenfalls im Jahr 2000 eingeweihte Stadthaus und Theater in Ijselstein, das ebenso wie die Kapelle mit Industrieglaswänden, Industriefassaden und Schulhausfenstern ganz pragmatisch seine Funktion erfüllt. Nur im Theatersaal werden mit blutroten Wänden und dunkelblauem Interieur Emotionen über atmosphärische Empfindungen geweckt.

Was sich bei der Müllentsorgungsstation in Delft andeutete, ist beim 1998 bezogenen Möbius-Haus in

An dieser Stelle ist eine Bemerkung zum Verhältnis Ben van Berkels zum Dekonstruktivismus angebracht. Er selbst will sich nicht als dekonstruktivistischer Architekt sehen. Keiner der philosophischen, keiner der künstlerischen Beweggründe für dekonstruktivistische Konzeptionen spielen bei ihm eine entscheidende Rolle. Der Kritiker Hubertus Adam hat einmal van Berkels Haltung angesichts des Möbius-Hauses mit einem Kunstvergleich deutlich gemacht. Van Berkels Konzeption verhalte sich zum Dekonstruktivismus wie der synthetische zum analytischen Kubismus. In der analytischen Phase des Kubismus würden wiedererkennbare Gegenstände in zersplit-

VILLA WILBRINK, AMERSFOORT (NL) VILLA WILBRINK, AMERSFOORT (NL) KAPELLE HILVERSUM (NL) CHAPEL HILVERSUM (NL) MÜLLENTSORGUNGSSTATION DELFT (NL) WASTE DISPOSAL FACILITY, DELFT (NL)

Het Gooi (▶72) schon manifest. Der Entwurf des Hauses gehorcht einem *Designmodell*, wie sie künftig in der Architektur von UNStudio eine Hauptrolle spielen werden. Das Haus ist nicht nur Funktion, es ist auch Konkretisierung eines Diagramms. Obwohl dieses auch die Belange der Funktion einer Regelung unterwirft, ist es nicht von dieser bestimmt und entfaltet zusätzlich eine semantische, eine narrative Dimension. In diesem Fall wurde die Möbius-Schleife – als Diagramm präsent – als räumliche Organisationsform des Hauses gewählt, freilich nicht in Reinform, sondern vielfältig gebrochen, nicht als signifikante Form, sondern als Ordnungsprinzip der Raumvektoren.

terter Form dargestellt. In der synthetischen sei der mimetische Aspekt verschwunden. Ebenso suche Ben van Berkel nach einer neuen Struktur, die Vielheit in Einheit überführe – und damit nach einer neuen Harmonie.

Vielleicht sollte man von vornherein besser den Konstruktivismusbegriff bemühen, der die Architektur zwischen Maschine und biologischem Organismus angesiedelt sehen wollte. Bei seiner Struktursuche verfolgt Ben van Berkel allerdings durchaus andere Wege als die Konstruktivisten, sei es deren funktionalistisch-technizistische Fraktion um Alexander Wesnin, sei es deren künstlerisch orientierte um El

and schoolroom windows. Only the blood red walls and dark blue interior of the theatre's auditorium stir emotion through the atmospheric quality that they create.

What is hinted at in the waste disposal facility in Delft manifests itself in the Möbius house in Het Gooi. (▸72) The design of this building is based on the design model that would become central to the architecture of UNStudio from that time onwards. Apart from its functionality, the building embodies a diagram. Although it also complies to the rules of function, it is not governed by them as it unfolds a semantic, narrative dimension. In this case, the Mö-

maintained that van Berkel's concept is to deconstructivism as the synthetic is to analytical cubism. Recognisable objects were portrayed in shattered form during the analytical stage of cubism. The mimetic aspect became lost in the synthetic. In the same manner, Ben van Berkel searched for a new structure to transfer multiplicity to unity—and therefore a new harmony.

Maybe the term deconstructivism, which placed architecture somewhere between machine and biological organism, should have been used from the beginning. However, in creating his structures, van Berkel travels other paths than the deconstructiv-

"LIGHTHOUSE", HAFENENTWICKLUNG, AARHUS (DK), RENDERING „LIGHTHOUSE" MIXED-USE HARBOUR DEVELOPMENT, AARHUS (DK), RENDERING WORLD BUSINESS CENTER BUSAN (KR), RENDERING WORLD BUSINESS CENTER BUSAN (KR), RENDERING URBAN OASIS SINGAPUR (SGP) URBAN OASIS SINGAPORE (SGP)

bius band—known in diagram form—was chosen to facilitate the spatial organisation of the house; not in its purest form nor as a clear form. It has been multiply divided, acting as a principle of order of the spatial vectors.

A comment on Ben van Berkel's relationship to deconstructivism would be appropriate here. He does not consider himself a deconstructivist architect. None of the philosophical nor creative motives behind deconstructivism are of great significance to him. The critic Hubertus Adam once offered an explanation of van Berkel's attitude towards the Möbius house using a comparison to the arts. He

ists did, whether their technical-functional fraction around Alexander Wesnin or the more art-oriented members around El Lissitzky. Driven by an insatiable curiosity for structural forms, Ben van Berkel collects diagrams. It seems that there are no ideas, no sciences, and no places on this earth that do not provide him with something; the flow pattern around a space shuttle, the armour pattern of a grain silo, the acoustic profile of Sydney Opera House, the script of a choreography, the notes of a piece of contemporary music, an electrical switch plan, the list goes on. He draws from this collection, similar to the way in which Oswald Mathias Ungers discovered morpho-

Lissitzky. Getrieben von einer unbändigen Neugier nach strukturellen Formen sammelt Ben van Berkel Diagramme. Es scheint keine Ideenwelt, keine Wissenschaft und keinen Ort auf dieser Welt zu geben, wo er nicht fündig wurde. Das Strömungsbild um eine Weltraumfähre, das Bewehrungsmuster eines Getreidesilos, das akustische Profil des Opernhauses in Sydney, das Skript einer Choreografie, die Struktur eines Enzyms, die Notation eines Stücks Neuer Musik, ein elektrischer Schaltplan, die Liste ließe sich fortsetzen.

Aus diesem Fundus schöpft er, ähnlich wie Oswald M. Ungers in seiner Sammlung morphologischer Strukturen Vorbilder für City-Metaphern ausfindig machte. Er findet Diagramme, die zunächst scheinbar nichts mit der Bauaufgabe zu tun haben und sich dann doch zu deren räumlicher und funktionaler Organisation tauglich erweisen.

Oft scheitern ambitionierte Architekten an dem Versuch, solcherart „architekturfremde" Parameter zum Hauptthema ihres Entwurfs zu machen, es bleibt bei der fixen Idee, die sich nicht legitimieren lässt. Anders bei UNStudio, dem es immer gelingt, auch den anderen Entwurfsparametern entsprechend Geltung zu verschaffen. Ihre Bauten sind immer eine Kombination, man möchte wegen des poetischen Gehalts eher sagen: eine Komposition aus Konzept, Funktion, Kontext und Expressivität. Darin unterscheidet sich van Berkel von Zeitgenossen seiner Architektengeneration, die man der Avantgarde zurechnet: Es ist die Gleichwertigkeit und Ausgewogenheit, mit der konzeptuelles Designmodell, nutzungsbezogene Struktur und dem Kunstwollen verhaftete Form miteinander in Beziehung gesetzt sind.

*Deep planning* nennen die Architekten ihren Ansatz, im Planungsprozess vor allem bei städtebaulichen Projekten alle funktionalen, strukturellen, aber auch politischen und wirtschaftlichen Einflussfaktoren zu erfassen. Hinzu kommt der Faktor Zeit (*time-based planning*). *Mixed media* ist ein weiterer Schlüsselbegriff der Architektur aus dem UNStudio. Er beschreibt die Gesamtheit der physischen Erfahrungen der Architektur durch den Rezipienten, den Nutzer,

den Bewohner, wie sie durch die Wahrnehmung mit allen fünf Sinnen vermittelt werden.

Wer all diese Faktoren berücksichtigt, kann eigentlich beim Bauen nichts falsch machen. Freilich ist man lediglich auf dem richtigen Weg und vom Ideal weit entfernt, denn schließlich bleibt Architektur die komplexeste Aufgabe, mit der sich der Mensch auf Erden konfrontiert sieht. Jedes andere Arbeitsfeld, ob Teilchenphysik oder Komposition, Flugzeugbau oder Philosophie, ist dagegen eindimensional.

Weder die Denk- und Arbeitsmethoden noch die Vorlieben bilden für UNStudio prinzipiell irgendwelche Einschränkungen bezüglich der Bauaufgaben. Dass noch keine Fabrikanlage, keine Klinik zu entwerfen war, ist eher Zufall. Was natürlich mit wachsender Größe der Projekte auf UNStudio zukam, waren Hochhäuser, zunächst in bescheidenem Maßstab wie in Arnheim (▶106), dann in einer Größenordnung, wie sie in der internationalen *Premier League* von Abu Dhabi bis Taichung Normalität sind.

Gleich 500 Meter sollte es im koreanischen Busan mit dem World Business Center in die Höhe gehen. UNStudio erarbeitete 2006 einen Masterplan und einen Hochhausentwicklungsplan. Ziel des Wettbewerbs war es, ein Wahrzeichen für die Stadt und die Region zu entwerfen. Der Masterplan ist darauf angelegt, eine phasenweise Realisierung des Großprojekts mit stetiger Anbindung an die bestehende Umgebung zu ermöglichen, die eine ebenso ökonomisch abgesicherte wie nachhaltige Entwicklung gewährleistet. Maßgeblich für die Grundrisse der Hochhausfamilie war ein Designmodell, das von einem algorithmisch erzeugten mathematischen Modell rollender Kurven ausgeht und zu kreisförmigen Kernen führt, an deren Peripherie kleinere Kreise eingewoben sind wie die Blütenblätter bei einer Blume. Von Stockwerk zu Stockwerk sich kontinuierlich verändernd, ergibt das Schema bündelförmige, organisch anmutende Türme von großer Prägnanz.

Ein ähnlicher Wettbewerb wurde 2007 für Singapur bearbeitet. Urban Oasis ist ein innerstädtisches Entwicklungsprojekt mit Büronutzung, Handel, Hotels und Wohnungen, das aus vielen Richtungen im

logical structural archetypes for city metaphors in his own collection. He finds diagrams that appear to have nothing to do with the building task and then reveal themselves to be applicable to its spatial and functional organisation.

Ambitious architects often fail in their attempts to make parameters that are so foreign to architecture the main elements of their designs; the original idea remains, never legitimatising itself. UNStudio is different. The practice always manages to make sense of such foreign design parameters. Their buildings are always a combination or rather, to do more justice to their poetry, a composition of concept, function, context, and expressivity. That is how van Berkel differs from the other avant-garde architects of his generation. His secret lies in the parity and equilibrium with which conceptual design model, function-relevant structure, and form anchored in artistic ambition, are placed in relation to one another. The architects call their approach of registering all functional, structural, as well as political and economic factors within the planning process deep planning. The time dimension is added to that—time-based planning. Mixed media is a further keyword at UNStudio. It describes the entirety of physical experience in architecture by the recipients, the users, the inhabitants, as they are communicated through all five senses.

Whoever takes all of these factors into account cannot go wrong in the building process. One is certainly on the right path although still far away from an ideal world; architecture remains the most complex of all tasks with which human beings are confronted. All other fields, whether particle physics or composition, aircraft construction or philosophy, are one-dimensional in comparison.

Neither methods of thought nor work nor their own partiality cause any constraint for UNStudio as far as their building activity is concerned. It is mere coincidence that they have not yet designed a factory facility nor a clinic. As the size of the projects carried out by UNStudio grow, their repertoire has come to include high-rise buildings; originally more modest ones such as in Arnhem (▸106) and then of dimensions that have become the norm in international premier league dimensions, from Singapore to Hangzhou.

The practice went straight to 500 metres with the building of the World Business Centre in Korean Busan. In 2006, UNStudio compiled a master plan and a high-rise development plan for the city. The objective of the competition was to design a symbol of the city and region. The master plan of this large project has been structured to enable implementation in phases with constant connection to the already existing surroundings, thus guaranteeing economically secure and sustainable development. A design model was of great significance for the ground plans of these high-rise buildings. It was based on a mathematical model of rolling curves that originated from an algorhythm. The rolling curves lead to circular cores into whose peripheries smaller circles are woven like the petals of a flower. As it moves from level to level, changing continually, the pattern creates clustered, organic-seeming, distinctive towers.

A similar competition was executed for Singapore. Urban Oasis is an inner-city development project with office, retail, hotel, and residential function. It can be seen from all directions and provides panoramic views into the distance. Two fifty-storey towers rise from an urban park like plants from the earth. They absorb the shape of the park and translate it into a third dimension. The façades react with diversity to the tropical conditions through gardens, terraces, balconies, and sun and rain protection. They are understood to embody a climatic skin that mediates between inside and outside both optically and technologically. Both of the spectacular high-rise buildings with their peristaltic movements advertise the "urban oasis" at their feet; a centre of commerce and entertainment.

A further high-rise, a 146-metre-high "beacon" accentuates a development project in Danish Aarhus that should be completed by 2013. A traffic-free promenade will be established on Pier 4, where

Blickpunkt steht und selbst gute Aussichten bietet. Aus einem Stadtpark heraus wachsen zwei 50-geschossige Turmhäuser wie Pflanzen aus der Erde, die die Formen des Parks aufnehmen und in die dritte Dimension verlängern. Die Fassaden reagieren auf vielfältige Weise mit Gärten, Terrassen und Balkonen, Sonnen- und Regenschutz auf die tropischen Konditionen. Sie werden als Klimahaut verstanden, die optisch und klimatechnisch zwischen innen und außen vermittelt. Die beiden spektakulären Hochhäuser mit ihren peristaltischen Bewegungen werben weithin für die „städtische Oase" zu ihren Füßen, ein Zentrum für Kommerz und Unterhaltung.

Apartments ein- oder zweigeschossig, in Einzelfällen dreigeschossig organisiert und auf komplizierte Weise zum Turmkörper zusammengesteckt.

Die Aussicht ist so wichtig wie die Ansicht, meinen die Architekten, und haben entsprechend attraktive Fassaden mit in der Höhe variierenden Brüstungen entworfen, wodurch der Eindruck schematischen Stapelns vermieden wird (bei den benachbarten, zehngeschossigen Wohnhäusern wird dieser Effekt zusätzlich durch unterschiedlich weit ausschwingende Stockwerksplatten unterstützt). Nur wenigen Wohnhochhäusern gelingt es, das Wohnen als Programm so konsequent zum Ausdruck zu bringen.

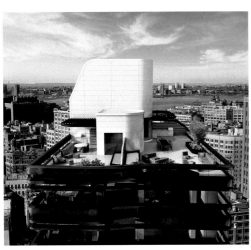

© Michael M

FIVE FRANKLIN PLACE, NEW YORK (USA), ANSICHT, PENTHÄUSER, WOHNRAUM (RENDERINGS) UND BAD FIVE FRANKLIN PLACE, NEW YORK (USA), VIEW, PENTHOUSES, LIVING ROOM (RENDERINGS) AND BATH

Ebenfalls ein Wohnhochhaus, ein 146 Meter hoher „Leuchtturm", akzentuiert ein Entwicklungsprojekt im dänischen Aarhus, das bis 2013 realisiert werden wird. Auf der Hafenpier 4, wo bislang Container gestapelt wurden, entstehen eine vom Verkehr befreite Promenade sowie privilegierte Wohnungen mit Sonne im Süden und einer wundervollen Aussicht auf das Kattegat im Osten und die Bucht Kale Vig im Norden. Die Nord-Ost-Spitze der Pier markiert ein Turmhaus mit Wohnungen und einem Aussichtscafé an der Spitze im 48. Stockwerk. Aus Gründen der ökonomischeren Erschließung der sehr unterschiedlich geschnittenen Wohnungen sind die

Sicher wird das auch dem ersten Projekt gelingen, das UNStudio in den USA realisiert. Five Franklin Place ist ein Hochhaus im Süden von Manhattan in der Nähe des Rockefeller Buildings. Auf 20 Geschossen sind teilweise zweigeschossige Loftwohnungen untergebracht, dazu ein privates Wellnessund Fitness-Center. Die Wohnungen der mittleren Geschosse haben Rundumsicht. Ebenso bieten die drei Penthäuser an der Spitze eine atemberaubende Aussicht auf die West Side und den Hudson River. Um dem Wohnhaus mit Apartments des oberen Preissektors zu einer besonderen, edleren Erscheinung zu verhelfen, umkleidet van Berkel das Gebäu-

shipping containers used to be stacked, as well as privileged apartments with sun from the south and a wonderful view of the Kattegat to the east and of Kale Vig Bay to the north. A forty-eight-storey tower building, accommodating apartments and a panorama café, will mark the north-eastern tip of the pier. In order to provide more financially viable access to the very diverse apartments, they have been arranged over one, two, and sometimes three storeys and pieced together in an extremely complicated manner to form the body of the tower.

According to the architects, the view is just as important as the elevation; they designed correspond-

a private spa and fitness centre. The apartments located towards its centre have panoramic views, and three penthouses at the top enjoy a breath-taking view of New York's West Side and the Hudson River.

In order to give this residential building with top of the range apartments a particularly noble appearance, van Berkel clad the building in black metal bands, "sewn on like the bordure of a luxury garment," as he puts it himself. The bands transform over their widths and turn the corner in gentle curves. They shape the building with strong sculptural relief, concealing its storey-structure.

IBG VERWALTUNGSZENTRUM, GRONINGEN (NL), RENDERING IBG & TAX OFFICE, GRONINGEN (NL), RENDERING LOUIS VUITTON FLAGSHIP STORE JAPAN, LOBBY UND ANSICHT, FOTO UND RENDERING LOUIS VUITTON FLAGSHIP STORE JAPAN, LOBBY AND VIEW, PHOTO AND RENDERING

ingly attractive façades with balustrades of varying heights that take away from a potential schematic stacking effect (in the design of the neighbouring ten-storey residential blocks the effect is further undermined by cantilevering slabs). Only a few high-rise buildings manage to differentiate themselves from office towers and to give expression to their residential function.

The first large-scale project that UNStudio will build in North America will also achieve that. Five Franklin Place is a high-rise building in TriBeCa, south Manhattan. Among other flats, loft apartments are accommodated in this twenty-storey building as is

It becomes obvious from the inside that these bands are directly related to interior layouts, functions, views and lighting. UNStudio also designed all of the bathrooms, kitchens, built-in wardrobes, and wooden furnishings, giving the building an unusually homogenous look.

The competition design for a Louis Vuitton flagship store in Japan is much more extroverted: it primarily aims to give the visitor the feeling of being in the world of Louis Vuitton by reflecting the qualities that are associated with the fashion brand.

The leaf shape moves through all levels of the design, establishing a connection to the famous LV

de mit schwarzen Metallbändern, „aufgenäht wie die Bordüren auf einem luxuriösen Gewand", wie er sich ausdrückt. Die Bänder wandeln sich in der Breite, umfangen die Ecken in sanfter Kurve und formen mit stark plastischem Relief einen Baukörper, der seine Stockwerksgliederung verschleiert.

In den Wohnungen wird deutlich, dass die Bänder direkt Bezug auf die innenräumlichen Verhältnisse, Nutzungen, Sicht- und Lichtverhältnisse nehmen. Das Design aller Bäder, Küchen, Wandschränke und hölzernen Einbauten kommt ebenfalls aus dem UNStudio, wodurch das Haus zu einer selten anzutreffenden gestalterischen Einheit wird.

skulpturalen Plastik wird, die inmitten stereometrischer Nachbarhäuser als Wahrzeichen erscheint.

Wie immer bei UNStudio ist nicht nur die Fassade, sondern das gesamte Haus vom Designmodell bestimmt. Alle Ebenen, Halbgeschosse, Treppenläufe, Wände und Wandöffnungen sind von einer gemeinsamen Bewegung durchdrungen, die das Flanieren im Haus zu einem unverwechselbaren Architektur- und damit Kauferlebnis macht. Unterschiedlich geschnittene und belichtete, hohe und enge Räume bieten abwechslungsreiche Möglichkeiten, die Produkte des Hauses zu präsentieren. Je höher der Besucher in dem Gebäude vordringt, desto intimer

THEATER, SPIJKENISSE (NL), ANSICHT, RENDERING THEATRE, SPIJKENISSE (NL), VIEW, RENDERING MOMEMA DUBAI (UAE), ZENTRALES FOYER MOMEMA DUBAI (UAE), CENTRAL FOYER

Deutlich extrovertierter gibt sich der Louis Vuitton Flagship Store in Tokio. Seine Architektur ist primär darauf angelegt, dem Besucher das ganzheitliche Gefühl zu vermitteln, sich in der Louis-Vuitton-Welt zu befinden, indem sie die Qualitäten widerspiegelt, die mit der Modemarke verbunden werden.

Durchgängiges Motiv ist die Blattform, die eine Verbindung zum berühmten LV-Monogramm herstellt. Diese Form wird überall im Haus angetroffen, in den Grundrissen, in den Räumen und bei den Fenstern. Die Blattform dominiert aber auch die plastische Ausformung des Baukörpers insgesamt, der auf diese Weise zu einer ungewöhnlichen, weiß strahlenden,

werden die Räume. Naturgemäß ist das Branding in diesem Fall die Hauptaufgabe der Architektur, bei einem Flagship Store durchaus plausibel.

Zu den Projekten, die sich ebenfalls auf dem Weg der Realisierung befinden, gehören so unterschiedliche Bauvorhaben wie das Bürohochhaus Mahler 4 an der Stadtautobahn im Süden Amsterdams oder der Umbau der Hauptpost in Rotterdam zu einem multifunktionalen Zentrum mit Handel, Büros und einem oben aufgesetzten Luxushotelturm.

Für die Informatie Beheer Groep und die regionale Finanzverwaltung entsteht in Groningen ein Verwaltungszentrum mit 42.000 Quadratmetern Bürofla-

monogram. It is to be found throughout the building; in the ground plans, the spaces, and the windows, also dominating the plastic formation of the building as a whole. The building becomes an unusual shining white sculpture of symbolic character in the midst of its stereometric neighbouring buildings.

As usual in the architecture of UNStudio, the whole building, rather than just the façade, has been defined by a design model. Its levels—mezzanines, staircases, walls and openings—are permeated by an overall movement, making a wander through the building a unique architectural and thus shopping

A 42,000 square-metre governmental administration centre is being built to accommodate 2,500 employees for the Informatie Beheer Groep and the regional fiscal authorities in Groningen. It is one of the largest public-private-partnership projects that the state building agency is involved in. The same actors will carry out design, building, finance and operation. A thirteen-storey tower surmounts the rounded twelve-storey building, which rises from an ameboid surface area. A pavilion of diverse function will complement this office complex, located in a park beside a motorway.

A new theatre of symbolic character is to be built

MOMEMA DUBAI (UAE), NORD- UND WESTANSICHT, RENDERINGS MOMEMA DUBAI (UAE), VIEWS FROM THE NORTH AND FROM THE WEST, RENDERINGS

experience. Diversely shaped and illuminated high and narrow spaces provide varied ways of presenting products. The higher the visitor climbs within the building, the more intimate the spaces become. In this case branding is the most important task of the architecture, which is certainly plausible in the case of a flagship store.

Other diverse projects that are also being built include the Mahler 4 office tower, situated on the new business centre beside the ring way of Amsterdam, and the conversion of the main post office in Rotterdam into a multifunctional centre of trade and offices, capped by a luxury hotel.

in the centre of Spijkenisse south of Rotterdam. A conventional auditorium and an experimental stage (black box) will be accessible from the foyer. The café on the glazed waterfront will have a significant role as the "third theatre," serving as a connecting element to the city. The dynamic shape of this building reacts with a bend and a curve to its uneven site. Its rounded shapes are intended to protect against wind turbulence, which could arise from a neighbouring historical windmill. Spijkenisse is a good example of the integrative function of an overall shape. The design thereby forms an antipode to the classical building structure according to Gottfried

che und 2500 Arbeitsplätzen. Es handelt sich um eines der ersten größeren PPP-Vorhaben der Staatlichen Bauagentur, bei dem Entwurf, Bau, Finanzierung und Betrieb in einer Hand blieben. Das allseits abgerundete, auf amöboider Grundfläche sich erhebende, zwölfgeschossige Gebäude wird von einem Turm mit weiteren 13 Geschossen überragt. Das Bürozentrum in einem Park an der Stadtautobahn wird ergänzt von einem Pavillon mit verschiedenen Nutzungen.

Das neue Theater der Stadt Spijkenisse im Süden Rotterdams wird in der Innenstadt gebaut und soll deshalb Wahrzeichencharakter bekommen. Ein konventioneller Theatersaal und eine Experimentalbühne (Black Box) sind vom zentralen Foyer aus zugänglich. Eine wichtige Rolle spielt als „drittes Theater" das Café an der gläsernen Wasserfront, das als verbindendes Glied zur Stadt fungiert. Die dynamische Form des Gebäudes reagiert mit Knick und Schwung auf das gekrümmte Baufeld. Die abgerundeten Formen sollen wegen der benachbarten historischen Windmühle Windturbulenzen vermeiden. Spijkenisse ist ein Beispiel für die integrative Funktion einer Großform. Der Entwurf steht damit im Gegensatz zur klassischen Baukörpergliederung nach Gottfried Semper, die Foyer, Zuschauerraum und Bühnenturm als Funktionseinheiten nach außen abbildet.

Durch die fließenden Linien und die wogenden Formen ergeben sich formale Verwandtschaften zu anderen UNStudio-Entwürfen, etwa zum Museum of Middle East Modern Art (MOMEMA), dessen Pläne für ein Grundstück in Dubai entstanden.

Ein Aspekt wird in Spijkenisse wie in Dubai deutlich. Obwohl diese Entwürfe oberflächlich betrachtet viel mit Zaha Hadids Architektur gemeinsam zu haben scheinen, ist die Großform nicht Selbstzweck, sondern steht in Beziehung zu den anderen Entwurfsparametern. Denn die Form des Theaters reagiert mit ihrer Asymmetrie auf funktionale und topologische Vorgaben. In Dubai wiederum ist die absolute Freiheit der selbstverliebten Form durch die gewählte Symmetrie diszipliniert, eine Symmetrie, die hier eindeutig als Würdeform fungiert. Diese Disziplin und

parametrische Einbindung enthebt die UNStudio-Entwürfe dem Ruch der formalen Beliebigkeit und ortlosen Unverbindlichkeit, die den spektakulären *signature buildings* der internationalen Avantgarde gegenwärtig anhaftet.

Mit dem MOMEMA soll in Dubai als Teil eines neuen „Culture Village" am Dubai Creek ein neuer Typus Kunstmuseum entstehen, mit Galerien, Künstlerateliers und Kunsthandel, mit Auditorium und Amphitheater, Hotel und Panoramarestaurant. Durch Veranstaltungen jeder Art, Handel, Unterhaltung und Erholung soll das Museum ein vibrierender Ort ständiger Aktivitäten und Ereignisse sein.

Welle, Delfin, Schiffsbug, gefrorene Bewegung – viele Assoziationen ruft das dynamische Gebäude hervor, für das es kein Vorbild zu geben scheint. Am Südende, in dem das Hotel untergebracht ist, läuft es elegant an, hebt vom Boden ab, tritt wieder auf und bäumt sich am Nordende zum Creek hin dramatisch auf. Stromlinien, vegetabile und maritime Elemente und die Formenrepertoires von avantgardistischen Yachten oder Rennwagen fließen ineinander zu einem atemberaubenden Designobjekt im Zyklopenmaßstab. Wie erwartet, gibt es im Inneren des Museums fließende Räume, keine Grenzen, Schwellen, nur ein Raum-Zeit-Kontinuum, in dem sich der Besucher auf sich selbst bezogen wiederfindet.

Der Entwurf ist noch unter den Idealbedingungen scheinbar unbegrenzter Möglichkeiten der Emirate entstanden und markiert einen Höhepunkt der architektonischen Agenda Ben van Berkels und des UNStudios. Und doch trifft auch für das Kunstmuseum in der Wüste zu, was für die Bauten in Europa galt. Die Komposition aus Konzept, Funktion, Kontext und Expressivität ist auch hier nachvollziehbar. Die Gleichwertigkeit und Ausgewogenheit, mit der das konzeptuelle Designmodell, die nutzungsbezogene Struktur und die dem Kunstwollen verhaftete Form miteinander in Beziehung gesetzt sind, ist auch dem Extrembeispiel Dubai zu eigen. So gesehen ist der Entwurf eine Weiterentwicklung des Musiktheaters in Graz (▶24), bei dem diese Ausgewogenheit heute schon erlebt werden kann.

Semper in which foyer, auditorium and stage tower are visible functional units from the outside.

The flowing lines and undulating shapes of this building establish a formal relationship to other UN-Studio designs such as the Museum of Middle East Modern Art (MOMEMA) which was planned for a plot in Dubai..

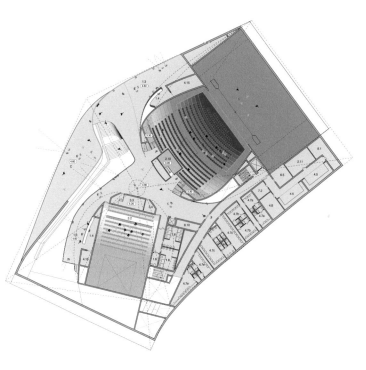

THEATER, SPIJKENISSE (NL), GRUNDRISS 1.OG THEATRE, SPIJKENISSE (NL), LAYOUT 1ST FLOOR

One factor is clear in both Spijkenisse and Dubai. Although these designs may appear on the surface to have a lot in common with the architecture of Zaha Hadid, an overall formal language has not been used just for the sake of it. It is clearly related to the other parameters of the designs. The theatre reacts with asymmetry to functional and topographical demands. In Dubai, the absolute freedom of the building's narcissistic form is disciplined by symmetry; clearly dignified symmetry. Such discipline and parametric integration, removes UNStudio designs from the realm of formal arbitrariness and non-committal placement currently associated with the spectacular signature buildings of the international avant-garde.

The MOMEMA in Dubai, part of a new "cultural village" at Dubai Creek, is planned to mark the birth of a novel type of art museum, incorporating galleries, artists' studios, art dealerships, an auditorium and amphitheatre, a hotel, and a panorama restaurant. Events of all kinds—retail, entertainment and leisure—will make the museum a vibrant location of constant activity and events.

The dynamic building awakens many associations—a wave, dolphin, the bow of a ship, a frozen movement—for which there appears to be no predecessor. At the southern end, in which the hotel is accommodated, the ground rises, steps down again and rises up dramatically towards the north end of the creek. Streamlines, elements from the vegetable and animal worlds, formal repertoires of avant-garde yachts or racing cars flow together to form a breath-taking design object of phenomenal scale. As to be expected, the interior of the building reveals flowing spaces—no limits, barriers, or ruptures—just a space-time continuum in which the visitor is reflected back upon himself.

The design had been created under the still ideal conditions of apparently unlimited potentials offered by the emirate and marks a climax and perhaps an endpoint of the architectural agenda of Ben van Berkel and UNStudio. However, the same can still be said of the art museum in the desert as of the European buildings. The composition of concept, function, context, and expressivity always remains comprehensible. The equality and balance with which conceptual design model, function-oriented structure, and artistically ambitious form have been placed in relation to one another is also a feature of the extreme Dubai project. From this point of view, the design is further developing the Music Theatre in Graz where this balance can already be experienced.

# PROJEKTE
# PROJECTS

# „MUMUTH", KUNSTUNIVERSITÄT, GRAZ (A)
# "MUMUTH," UNIVERSITY OF MUSIC AND PERFORMING ARTS, GRAZ (A)

Das Proben- und Aufführungsgebäude der Universität für Musik und darstellende Kunst Graz (Haus für Musik und Musiktheater „MUMUTH") ist ein Beispiel der Anwendung der Designmodelle von UNStudio. Das hier umgesetzte *blob-to-box model* beschreibt die Entwicklung des Baukörpers und des Raums von der Nordseite, der *box*, bis zur Südseite, dem *blob*, im Fall des Idealdiagramms die kontinuierliche morphologische Wandlung von einem rechtwinkligen, kartesischen zu einem frei geformten Volumen am anderen Ende. In der Realität hat die *box* mit Bühne und Zuschauerraum ein Zweidrittel-Übergewicht über die bewegteren Formen im Bereich des Foyers, deren gläserne Außenhaut sich wie unter Druck stehend nach außen wölbt.

Der Alltagseingang für den Lehrbetrieb befindet sich auf der Parkseite, der Abendeingang für das Publikum an der Straßenfront. Bei Veranstaltungen wird das Studentenfoyer zur Garderobe umfunktioniert. Eine Architektur aus Musik, ein Haus, das den akustischen Raum sichtbar macht, in dem Musik gelebt wird, erfährt der Besucher vor allem im Zuschauerbereich. Dramatisch schraubt sich die zentrale Treppe wie eine Spiralfeder im Foyer nach oben. „*Classical with a twist*" nennen es die Architekten, und bringen damit den Raum zum Schwingen. Im öffentlichen Bereich des Hauses wird die Bewegung des Publikums im fließenden, alles verbindenden Raum inszeniert. Die Spirale bringt die drei Ebenen zusammen, um sie dreht sich alles. Sie wird von einem Oberlicht beleuchtet, in dem sich silberfarbene Lamellen auffächern und ein dynamisches Wellenmuster bilden.

Die Wiederholung ist ein musikalisches Motiv, vor allem in der Neuen Musik, das Verdichtung, Intensivierung und Improvisation erlaubt. UNStudio hat deshalb ein repetitives Motiv gewählt, ausgeführt als Siebdruckmuster in gedeckten Tönen des Bühnen-Make-ups in verschiedener Intensität, mit dem die gläsernen Außenwände geschmückt sind. Das Dekor wandelt sich in der Erscheinung je nach Beleuchtung und Betrachtungswinkel im Zusammenspiel mit dem glitzernden Maschenwerk der äußeren Gebäudehülle.

This rehearsal and performance building at the University of Music and Performing Arts (Haus für Musik und Musiktheater „MUMUTH") in Graz, Austria, demonstrates how a UNStudio design model can be applied. The blob-to-box model used in this project traces the development of building and space from north side (box) to south side (blob). It morphologically mutates from a right-angled Cartesian shape at one end to a freely formed volume at the other. However, the box, containing stage and auditorium, is two-thirds larger in volume than the flowing forms of the foyer area, whose glass façade curves outwards as if under stress.

The everyday entrance for students and teachers is located on the car park side, while evening visitors enter the building from the street. During events, the students' foyer is converted into a cloakroom. Visitors experience architecture made of music, visible acoustic space, music alive; especially in the auditorium. The foyer's central staircase dramatically stretches upwards like a coiled spring. "Classical with a twist" is what the architects call it; they use it to make the space swing.

Audience movement through the building's public areas has been composed within a flowing space that connects different areas to each other. The spiral links all three levels; everything revolves around it. At its apex light enters through a skylight, on which silver coloured lamellas fan out to create a dynamic wave pattern. Such repetition is a musical motif, particularly from classical twentieth and twenty-first century music; it facilitates densification, intensification, and improvisation. The architects therefore chose a repetitive design. They have applied it as a silk screened pattern, in the muted tones of stage make-up in varying degrees of intensity, in the composition of the building's external glass walls. It changes its appearance depending on the lighting and viewpoint, interacting with the sparkling meshwork of the external cladding.

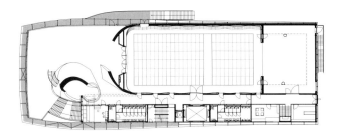

# MUSEUM HET VALKHOF, NIMWEGEN (NL)
# HET VALKHOF MUSEUM, NIJMEGEN (NL)

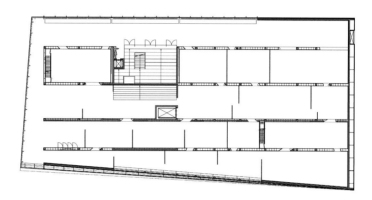

Einst stand auf dem Gelände am Rand der Altstadt ein Römerlager, dann eine karolingische Burg, später lagen hier die romanischen Wallanlagen, die sich heute noch in einem Grüngürtel um die Stadt abzeichnen. Hinter dem grünen Wall rauscht der Verkehr des Autobahnzubringers gen Arnheim, nach Norden weitet sich der Blick zum Ufer der Waal.

Für das neue Museum war hier eine große Geste gefragt, und die Architekten antworteten entsprechend großzügig auf die Situation mit einer breiten Front, die durch schmale Glasbänder und zwei knappe Geschossvorsprünge eine kaum merkliche Horizontalgliederung erhielt. Eine Phalanx von 13 Türen öffnet den Weg von Rampe und Freitreppe ins Innere des Hauses, während ein weitläufiger dreieckiger Platz die Distanz zur kleinteiligen Altstadt hält.

Wie von einem Sog wird der Besucher im Foyer von der zweigeteilten breiten Treppenanlage ins Obergeschoss gezogen. Die suggestive Wirkung entsteht durch lange, flache, hellblau gestrichene

A Roman camp was once located on this site at the edge of the old town, then a Carolingian Castle and Roman ramparts, the outlines of which are still traced by a greenbelt around the city today. Traffic races by towards Arnhem along a motorway approach road, which runs behind the green embankment; the view opens to the north towards the banks of the River Waal.

A grand gesture was called for in the building of this new museum. The architects responded appropriately to the situation with a wide front of subtle horizontal structure defined by narrow glass bands and two slight shifts forward between the levels. A thirteen-door phalanx opens the way from a ramp and stairway into the building, while a roomy, three-cornered square preserves the distance to the old town of smaller scale structure.

The visitor is pulled into the foyer and onto the top floor, as if by suction, by a wide two-tiered staircase. The suggestive effect is created by long, flat concrete steps painted light blue and mighty bal-

Betonstufen und mächtige Brüstungen aus hellem Massivholz. Die geschwungene Deckenverkleidung aus Aluminiumlamellen verstärkt den Effekt. Die Treppe führt hinauf zur rückseitigen Galerie, die sich auf ganzer Breite ins Grüne öffnet und andererseits die Schauräume erschließt.

Es war die Absicht, die sehr heterogenen Sammlungen des Provinzialmuseums G. M. Kam und des Museums Commanderie van Sint-Jan mit Exponaten von römischen Münzfunden über Kunstgewerbe verschiedener Epochen bis zur Malerei der Gegenwart nicht zu separieren, sondern sie als gesamtheitliche Kulturleistung erlebbar zu machen. Es gibt deswegen keinen Zwangsrundgang.

ustrades of light-coloured massive wood. Curved ceiling cladding of aluminium lamellas underlines this effect. The staircase leads directly to a rear gallery, which opens out towards the green landscape along the whole width of the building while also providing access to the exhibition spaces.

The objective of this project was to unite rather than to separate the extremely heterogeneous collections of the more local G. M. Kam Museum and the Commanderie van Saint-Jan Museum with exhibits ranging from Roman coins to art spanning several centuries to contemporary paintings; allowing visitors to experience them as a holistic cultural collection.

Die Museumsdidaktik geht von einem unkonventionellen, gewissermaßen informellen Ordnungsprinzip aus. Die Besucher werden zu Suchern und finden ihren Weg durch die in vier Reihen hinter- und nebeneinander gereihten Schauräume, begleitet von der auf- und abwogenden Decke und je nach Gusto von einem Saal zum nächsten oder über die Querverbindungen zu den Nachbarsälen flanierend. Sehr helle Farben und viel Licht verleihen dem Raumkontinuum Großzügigkeit und prägen den besonderen Charakter der Ausstellungsräume.

There is no one circuit of the museum; it is didactically based on an unconventional, relatively informal principle of order. Visitors become explorers as they find their way through the exhibition spaces, which have been positioned in four rows, one after the other. Accompanied by the up and down waves of the ceiling, they wander from one room to the next as they please or to a neighbouring room via cross connections. The grandesse of this spatial continuum results from very light colours and much light, which define the special character of the exhibition rooms.

# MERCEDES-BENZ MUSEUM, STUTTGART (D)

Das Automobilmuseum neu zu definieren, war UNStudio in Stuttgart angetreten. Anlass war die Absicht der ersten Autoschmiede der Welt, den unscheinbaren Museumsbau mitten im Werksgelände durch einen Neubau zu ersetzen. 500.000 Besucher jährlich hatte die weltweit älteste Automobilsammlung zuvor schon, inzwischen sind es über eine Million, die das allererste Automobil, das erste Motorrad und das erste Motorboot von Carl Benz, den ersten LKW, dazu Rekordfahrzeuge dutzendweise, wunderschöne Karossen der dreißiger Jahre, Silberpfeile und Formel-1-Boliden sehen wollen. Nun ließ Daimler dafür ein Museum der Superlative bauen, einen „Ort für den Mythos", ein „Heritage Center" der traditionsreichen Autofabrik. UNStudio hatte den internationalen Architektenwettbewerb mit einem Entwurf gewonnen, der dem Bauherrn das gewünschte Maß an Innovation, Extravaganz und Attraktion versprach.

Der Neubau fand seinen Platz vor der Hauptpforte des Stammwerks Untertürkheim auf einer topografisch geformten Plattform, unter der Parkplätze, aber auch Gastronomie und Läden untergebracht sind. Neben einer Hochstraße reckt sich der kompakte, pulsierende Bau in die Höhe und verschafft sich weithin optisch Geltung. Außen zeigt er eine schimmernde Silberpfeilkarosserie, deren Rundformen und wogende Aluminiumbänder sich der Logik einer erkennbaren Stockwerkseinteilung verweigern und deren aus- und eingekippte Fensterbahnen in Bewegung zu sein scheinen.

Im Inneren ergeben sich attraktive Raumfolgen, immer neue räumliche Konstellationen und Verbindungen, die einem raffinierten Ordnungsprinzip gehorchen. Ingenieure und Bautechniker waren aufs Äußerste gefordert, denn die Architekten fühlten sich bei ihrer Raumerfindung nicht an statische Gesetze gebunden. Bis auf die Innenwände der Aufzugsschächte gibt es im Haus keine Wand, die nicht gebogen wäre; viele Wände sind gar zweiachsig gekrümmt, eine enorme Herausforderung für die Betonbauer, die ihre Schalungen von der Computerfräse erstellen lassen mussten. Ohne

UNStudio came to Stuttgart to redefine the Automobile Museum. The brief was to replace the world's first car workshop, a modest museum building right at the heart of the plant grounds, with a new building. The world's oldest collection of cars attracted 500,000 visitors per year, a figure which has recently risen to over one million. People come to see the first motorbike and the first motorboat by Carl Benz, the first truck and dozens of special vehicles, beautiful car bodies dating back to the 1930s, Silver Arrows and Formula 1 bolides. Daimler has now had a museum built, a "place to house the myth," a heritage center for the tradition-steeped car factory. UNStudio won the international architectural competition with a design that promised the client the desired proportions of innovation, extravagance and attraction.

The new building was positioned before the front gates of the Untertürkheim main plant on a topographical platform under which parking spaces as well as catering and shops have been accommodated. The compact, pulsating building stretches into the air beside a flyover, attracting attention from far and wide. On the outside it demonstrates gleaming silver arrow body work whose rounded shapes and wavy bands of aluminium defy the logic of recognisable storeys and whose strip windows, which lean alternately in and out, appear to be in motion.

The inside spaces embody attractive, repeatedly novel spatial constellations and connections, which bow to a refined principle of order. Engineers and building technicians were challenged to their limits as the architects did not allow themselves to be bound by the laws of statics in their creation of these spaces. Apart from the walls of the elevator shafts, there is not one straight wall in the building. Many of them have even been bent about two axes, a huge challenge to the concrete workers whose formwork was made by a computerized moulding cutter. The complex structure could never have been mastered without the most advanced computer programs. Thirty five thousand plans were required for the

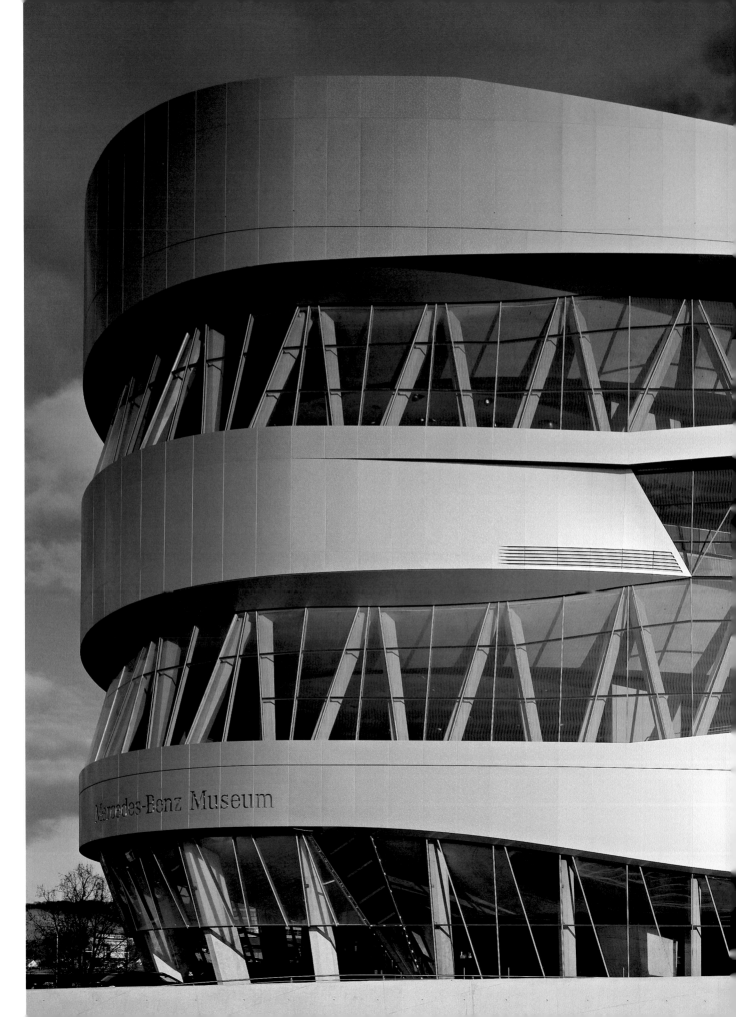

avancierteste Computerprogramme wäre die komplexe Raum- und Konstruktionsstruktur ohnehin nicht zu meistern gewesen; 35.000 Pläne waren zum Bau notwendig und viele Handwerker mussten erst die Arbeit nach einem Computermodell erlernen.

Als „Doppelhelix" wird das einem mathematischen Programm, einer komplexeren Form des Möbius-Bandes entsprechende Erschließungsprinzip beschrieben, zwei ineinander verwobene Spiralen, die von oben gesehen die Form eines Kleeblatts bilden. Um die zentrale dreieckige, haushohe Foyerhalle gruppieren sich in fünf Ebenen die „Blätter", die halbkreisförmigen Schauräume. Es gibt solche mit Kunstlicht und solche mit natürlichem Licht und prächtiger Aussicht ins Neckartal.

Die Besucher werden von gläsernen Aufzügen auf die oberste Ebene gebracht. Während der Fahrt erleben sie eine Multimediashow. Oben erwartet sie die Geburtsstunde des Automobils, wonach sie die weitere Geschichte auf dem Rampenweg entlang der Spiralen nach unten verfolgen können. Einer der gewundenen, immerhin 1,8 Kilometer langen Wege verbindet die inneren Räume miteinander, die „Mythosräume" mit von dem Stuttgarter Architekten HG Merz aufwändig gestalteten Inszenierungen, in denen in chronologischer Folge die Firmengeschichte erzählt wird. Wer die andere Spirale wählt, durchwandert die Sammlungsräume, in denen einzelne Aspekte (helfen und retten, reisen, Transport etc.) thematisiert werden. Da sich die Räume vielfach miteinander verschränken, gibt es Querverbindungen zwischen den Spiralen und somit anregende atmosphärische Wechsel zwischen Sonnenglanz und Theaterlicht, befreiender Aussicht und bühnenreifen Szenarien. Beide Wege enden auf der unteren Ebene der „Rennen und Rekorde", wo die spektakulärsten und sicher beliebtesten Ausstellungsstücke aus 110 Jahren Mercedes-Renngeschichte auf einer Steilkurve zu bestaunen sind. Der Weg im Tiefparterre führt vorbei an den Boxen, in denen die Erforschung neuer Techniken und Materialien für den Automobilbau didaktisch interessant aufbereitet ist und weiter zum Amphitheater, zur Passage mit dem Brand Shop und dem Restaurant, wo der Rundgang zum Ende kommt.

Das Mercedes-Benz Museum ist das vorerst komplexeste und bedeutendste Bauwerk aus dem UNStudio, bei dem der Bauherr den Architekten weitgehend folgte und es ihnen ermöglichte, ein Konzept konsequent von der mathematisch-theoretischen Idee bis zum fertigen Bauwerk zu entwickeln und mit nicht geringem Aufwand zu realisieren. Das Ergebnis ist im Inneren ein unvergleichliches Raumkontinuum und von außen eine Ikone, mit der sich der Auftraggeber schmücken kann.

building and many of the workmen had to learn to work using a computer model for the first time.

The communication principle within the building is described by mathematical programmes as a, "double helix". It is a more complex type of Möbius band, which results in two intertwining spirals that form a cloverleaf shape when seen from above. The five "leaves," the semi-circular exhibition spaces, are grouped on five levels around a central triangular foyer hall, which extends the entire height of the building. Some are lit artificially while others are lit naturally with a wonderful view into the Neckar Valley.

Glazed elevators transport visitors to the top most level, during which they see a multi-media presentation. At the top they are greeted by the moment of creation of the automobile after which they learn about its historical development as they follow the ramp down through the spiral. One of the winding 1.8 metre-long ramps connects the inner spaces with each other. These are the "mythical spaces" created in conjunction with Stuttgart's HG Merz Architects to accommodate elaborately designed presentations of the history of the company in chronological order. Those who choose the other spiral wander through the collection spaces in which individual aspects (helping people and saving lives, travel, transport, etc.) are focussed upon. Since the spaces repeatedly intertwine, there are cross connections between the spirals and thus stimulating shifts in atmosphere between sunshine and theater lighting, liberating views, and stage set scenarios. Both paths end on the bottom level of "Races and Records" where the most spectacular and most popular exhibition pieces from 110 years of Mercedes racing history can be wondered at on a racing loop. The path to the half-basement leads past boxes in which research on new technologies and materials for car manufacturing is presented in a didactically interesting manner; it continues to the amphitheater, the brand shop and the restaurant, where the tour ends.

So far the Mercedes-Benz Museum is the most complex and significant structure to have been built by UNStudio, a project in which the client largely adhered to the ideas of the architects, allowing them to consistently develop a concept from the mathematical-theoretical idea to the finished structure; no uncomplicated structure to build. The result is a unique spatial continuum on the inside and an icon from the outside, with which the client has certainly made its mark.

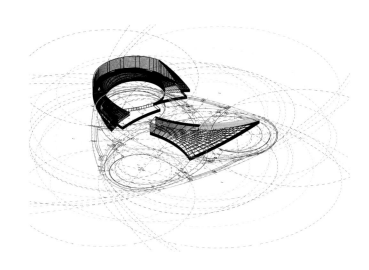

# TEEHAUS AUF EINEM BUNKER, VREELAND (NL)
# TEA HOUSE ON BUNKER, VREELAND (NL)

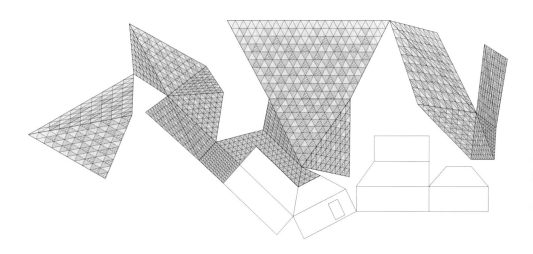

Was tun mit einem Bunker aus dem Jahr 1936, der nutzlos zwischen den Baulichkeiten eines Poloclubs vor sich hinträumt und als Kulturdenkmal nicht zur Disposition steht? Der Bauherr, ein Fördermitglied des Poloclubs, veranstaltete einen kleinen Ideenwettbewerb und beauftragte dann UNStudio mit der ungewöhnlichen Aufgabe.

Van Berkel greift die Form auf, expandiert sie, faltet sie auf, lässt sie aufsteigen und bedenklich vorkragen und schneidet sie ganz abrupt ab. Diese nach Südwesten blickende breiteste Stelle des vorwitzig auskragenden Baukörpers, vom Boden bis zur Decke voll verglast, ist offenbar die Quintessenz des Baus. Von innen gesehen wird deutlich warum: Der 80 Quadratmeter große Raum funktioniert wie eine privilegierte Loge, öffnet sich zum Vorreitplatz und zum Spielfeld hin. Von hier aus genießt man aus sicherer Warte bei einer Tasse Tee den besten Blick auf das Treiben vor und auf dem Polofeld.

What to do with a bunker built in 1936? A cultural monument standing between the buildings of a polo club, it had to stay. The client, a sponsor of the polo club, organised a small competition and then commissioned UNStudio with an unusual project.

Van Berkel works with form, expands it, unfolds it, lets it rise and jut out precariously before cutting it off abruptly. The widest part of this daringly protruding building faces south west, is glazed from top to bottom, and is clearly the quintessence of the whole, a fact that becomes clear from the inside. The space, measuring 80 square-metres, resembles a privileged lodge in function, opening out towards the exercise track and the polo field. One can enjoy an optimal view of activities in front of and on the polo field over a cup of tea from this safe observatory location.

The bunker is merely the grain from which this budding form unfolds. There is nothing sweet about it, leading the architect to proceed in hard, aggressive shapes. The cement block remains almost

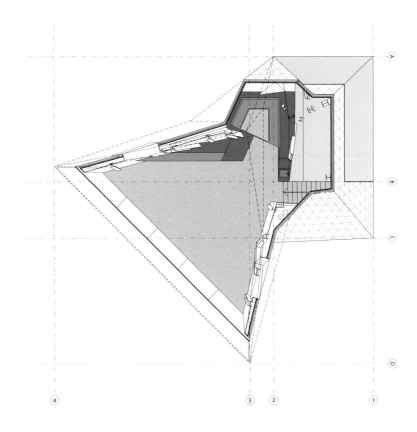

Der Bunker ist nur das Samenkorn, aus dem sich die knospende Form entfaltet. Er hat nichts Liebliches, und so denkt ihn der Architekt weiter in harten, aggressiven Formen. Der Betonblock bleibt fast unberührt, bildet mit seiner betagten, rauen und berankten Oberfläche einen rüden Kontrast zur blinkenden Edelstahlhaut des Aufbaus. Sein Inneres wird nicht genutzt. Der Zugang zum Teehaus erfolgt als Sesam-öffne-dich durch eine Schiebewand im Anbau und über eine schmale Treppe hinauf in den sich mit großer Geste überraschend öffnenden Raum. Der ganze Bau ist Inszenierung, springt in die Höhe, entfaltet sich explosionsartig; der Bau ist nichts als kostbar präsentierte Aussicht, als gäbe es an diesem Ort nur diese, und nichts auf der Welt kann wichtiger sein.

untouched and, with its old, rough, ivy-covered surface, stands in crude contrast to the new structure's sparkling stainless steel skin. The space inside the bunker is unused. A sliding door in the building extension forms the entrance to the tea house with "Open Sesame!" like effect. It leads up a narrow staircase where the space unexpectedly opens out with an expansive gesture. The entire building is performance; it leaps into the air and unfolds explosively. It serves no other purpose than to present this precious view, as if there were nothing else in this place and nothing in the world of greater importance.

# NMR KERNSPINRESONANZ-LABOR, UTRECHT (NL)
# NMR FACILITY, UTRECHT (NL)

Für die Spektroskopie von Kernspinresonanzphänomenen sind starke Hochfrequenzmagnete notwendig, die besondere Bedingungen an ein Laborgebäude stellen. Einerseits benötigen die Geräte einen genügend großen Abstand zueinander, um die Messergebnisse nicht gegenseitig zu beeinflussen, andererseits gilt es, die Ausbreitung von Magnetstrahlung nach außen zu verhindern.

Inspiriert durch die von dem sächsischen Mathematiker Herbert Seifert definierten Seifert-Flächen erdachten die Architekten ein System der umwickelnden Betonflächen. Fußböden falten sich auf zu Wänden und weiter zu Decken und umhüllen die Räume wie der Teig die Füllung im Apfelstrudel. Es entstanden zweigeschossige, stützenfreie Räume, in denen die acht Spektroskope Aufstellung fanden. Die fensterlose Betonummantelung sorgt für die Abschirmung der Magnetfelder. Nebenräume, Labors und Büros sind außen angefügt. Auf einen Lift hat man wegen dessen elektromagnetischem Störpotenzial verzichtet. Die Lastandienung für das Obergeschoss geschieht über eine außen angebaute Rampe.

Die äußere Erscheinung des Laborgebäudes ist von zwei Materialien bestimmt: den Betonflächen, die sich um das Gebäude schmiegen, es durchdringen und es bedecken, sowie von den mehrheitlich rahmenlosen Glasflächen, mit denen die Geschosse geschlossen sind und durch die die umlaufende Rampe nach außen geschützt ist.

Wie so oft haben die Architekten ein mathematisch-geometrisches Prinzip einerseits und die Nutzungsanforderungen andererseits für die Konzeption und Gestaltung des Gebäudes verwandt. Ein weiteres Mal haben sie den Versuch unternommen, die Dichotomie zwischen Boden, Wand und Decke zu überwinden und kontinuierliche Strukturen anzubieten, die sich in ihrer Anmutung vom Bild eines konventionellen Hauses weit entfernen, ohne es jedoch in die Nähe der Beliebigkeit und Nutzungsproblematik der Blob-Architektur zu drängen.

Strong high-frequency magnets are required for nuclear magnetic resonance spectroscopy; these demand particular conditions of a laboratory building. There must be a minimum amount of distance between them so that they cannot influence each other, while precautions must also be taken to prevent magnetic radiation from spreading outwards.

Inspired by "Seifert Surfaces" as defined by the German mathematician Herbert Seifert, the architects invented a system of wrapped concrete surfaces. Floors fold to become walls and further into ceilings, surrounding the spaces as the pastry of apple strudel does the filling. Two-storey, column-free spaces emerged in which the eight spectroscopes could be installed. The windowless concrete envelope manages to contain the magnetic fields. Service rooms, laboratories and offices are connected to them on the exterior. No elevator was installed due to the risk of electromagnetic interference that it would bring. Heavy deliveries are made to the top floor via an exterior ramp.

The outer appearance of the laboratory building is defined by two materials; the concrete surfaces that wrap themselves around the building, penetrate, and cover it and the predominantly frameless glass surfaces that seal the various storeys and protect the circumferential ramp from the elements.

The architects have yet again applied a mathematical-geometrical principle coupled with the functional requirements of the building to come up with a concept and design for this building. They have once more undertaken an experiment with which to overcome the dichotomy between floor, wall, and ceiling, producing continuous structures that remain far-removed from traditional concepts of the traditional building without entering blob architecture territory and the arbitrariness and functional problems that come with it.

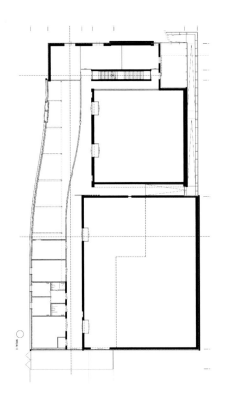

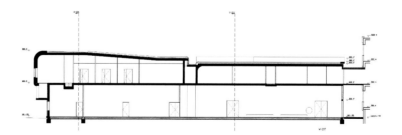

# PRINZ-CLAUS-BRÜCKE, UTRECHT (NL)
# PRINCE CLAUS BRIDGE, UTRECHT (NL)

Die Erasmusbrücke bekam eine Schwester, die Prinz-Claus-Brücke in Utrecht über den Amsterdam-Rhein-Kanal. Zwar ist sie mit 91 Metern Pylonhöhe und 115 Metern Spannweite wesentlich kleiner, doch die Verwandtschaft ist nicht nur wegen der hellblauen Farbgebung, sondern auch wegen des schrägen Pylons und der Schrägseilharfe offenkundig. Allerdings sind die Ankerkabel für den Gegenzug ebenfalls als Schrägseilharfe ausgeführt, weshalb die Brücke nicht den entschiedenen Richtungscharakter hat wie die Erasmusbrücke.

Der Pylon wächst aus einem dynamischen Stützbock heraus, stößt zwischen den Fahrbahnen nach oben und schießt wie ein Amaryllistrieb in die Höhe. Dabei verändert er seinen quadratischen Querschnitt kontinuierlich, bis er in einer schlanken Keule mit ovaler Spitze endet. Diese techno-organische Metamorphose verleiht dem Pylon Eleganz und Charakteristik. Auch die Spannkabel tragen zu dieser Wirkung bei, denn die Ansatzpunkte ihrer Verankerung am Pylon bilden eine elegante Ellipse.

Durch die Formgebung jenseits simplifizierender statischer Bedingungen und Vorgaben gelingt es, die reale und die imaginäre Erfahrung des Brückenschlags als spannungsreiche Bewegung auch in der Realität der stählern-technischen Bewältigung hoher Lasten und Kräfte zum Ausdruck zu bringen und die Wahrnehmung der Brücke als organische Leistungsform zu ermöglichen. Dies ist umso bemerkenswerter, als die Brücke durch einen Generalunternehmer zum Festpreis gebaut worden ist und dieser bei der Gestaltung und Detailausbildung freie Hand hatte. Den Architekten gelang es jedoch, frühzeitig ein schlüssiges Konzept zu liefern, das Gestaltung und Konstruktion integrativ vereinte und gravierende Veränderungen (die üblicherweise zur Banalisierung führen) nicht mehr zuließ.

The Erasmus Bridge has been given a sister in the shape of the Prince Claus Bridge over the Amsterdam-Rhine Canal in Utrecht. Although it is much smaller at a pylon height of 91 metres and a span of 115 metres, their kinship is obvious, finding expression in the slanting pylon, the harp of slanted cables and not least its light blue color. However, the counter-balancing anchor cables are formed by another harp of slanted cables so that this bridge does not demonstrate as decisive an orientation as the Erasmus Bridge does.

The pylon originates from a dynamic pedestal; it rises between the carriageways, shooting like an amaryllis bud into the air. As it does so, its square profile alters continually to end in a slender pin with an oval pinnacle. This technological-organic metamorphosis gives the pylon elegance and character. The tension cables also contribute; the holding points of their anchorage to the pylon form an elegant ellipse.

The profile of the bridge, which does more than simply fulfil static conditions, gives expression to a real and imagined bridge experience; a tension-filled movement despite the current reality in which high loads and forces can be technologically mastered with ease, allowing the powerful organic system that it embodies to be perceived. This is even more remarkable as the bridge was erected at a fixed rate by a general contractor who had the freedom to do as he saw fit throughout the implementation phase. However, the architects managed to provide a coherent concept that united design and construction in the early stages of planning, thus ruling out any further major changes (which could otherwise have led to mundanity).

# ERASMUSBRÜCKE, ROTTERDAM (NL)
# ERASMUS BRIDGE, ROTTERDAM (NL)

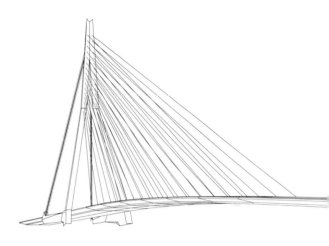

Der Philosoph Erasmus von Rotterdam ist Namenspatron der Brücke über die Neue Maas. Die Brücke verbindet das Geschäftszentrum Rotterdams mit dem südlich der Maas liegenden Hafengebiet „Kop van Zuid", das seit zwei Jahrzehnten nach und nach mit Dienstleistungs- und Wohnquartieren bebaut wird. Dort im Süden entwickelte sich ein neues Kraftfeld Rotterdams und so suchte die Stadt nach einem emblematischen Bindeglied über die Neue Maas, das Alt und Neu physisch und symbolisch miteinander in Beziehung setzt. Der Entwurf für die insgesamt 800 Meter lange „Nieuwe Stadsbrug" von Ben van Berkel und Caroline Bos aus dem Jahr 1989 versprach die gewünschten technizistischen und skulpturalen Qualitäten zu bieten und wurde im Wettbewerb ausgewählt.

Von Süden her überspannt das Bauwerk den Fluss bis hinüber zur dicht bebauten Innenstadt und scheint dort ganz sanft aufzusetzen. Die schlanke Fahrbahn hängt an einer Harfe von 32 Schrägseilen, der 139 Meter hohe Pylon stemmt sich sichtlich gegen ihren Zug. Breitbeinig steht er über den Fahrbahnen im Wasser. Zur anderen Seite hin ist er mit acht mächtigen Zugseilen rückverankert. Die abstrakte Figur Gullivers, der nach beiden Seiten die Balance hält, kniet dort am Hafen, so hat es den Anschein.

Ingenieurleistung und architektonischer Entwurf sind eine fruchtbare Symbiose eingegangen, um ein Bauwerk zu kreieren, das in technischer, gestalterischer und philosophischer Eleganz das trennende Wasser überwindet; das die Herkulesaufgabe der 280 Me-

This bridge over the New Maas River has been named after the philosopher Erasmus from Rotterdam. It connects the commercial center of Rotterdam with the "Kop van Zuid" port area to the south of the River Maas, on which service and residential areas have gradually been established over the last two decades. The area to the south of the river was developing into one of Rotterdam's core areas, which lead the city to go in search of a novel symbolic connecting element over the New Maas to join new and old to each other. The design for an 800-metre long bridge, the "Nieuwe Stadsbrug" by Ben van Berkel and Caroline Bos, won a competition held in 1989 as it promised to deliver the desired technological and sculptural qualities.

The bridge spans the river from the south over to the dense inner city, where it appears to touch down very softly. Its slender deck hangs from a harp of thirty-two slanted cables. A 139-metre-high pylon obviously braces itself against their pull; it stands over the carriageways, legs apart in the water, anchored to the other side by eight powerful load cables. An abstract figure of Gulliver appears to keep things in balance as it kneels down on both sides the harbor.

A symbiosis of engineering know-how and architectural design have produced a volume that transcends the separating water in its technological, artistic, and philosophical elegance. This bridge masters the incredible challenge of spanning a distance of 280 metres with ease while arousing a sense of the vibrating tension

er Hauptspannweite mit Leichtigkeit meistert und trotzdem die
ibrierende Spannung erahnen lässt, unter der die filigranen Teile
tehen. In einem hellen Blau gestrichen, machen sich Pylon und
eile dem Himmel anverwandt. Und selbst die schweren Sockel
er Widerlager, die Rampen und Brüstungen aus Beton zeigen von
er Bewegung bestimmte dynamische Formen. Der südlich an-
chließende Brückenteil ist als Hubbrücke ausgeführt und kann für
e Durchfahrt von Schiffen geöffnet werden. Er gilt als schwerste
lappbrücke Westeuropas.

b ihrer Zeichenhaftigkeit und Eleganz ist die des Nachts effektvoll
uminierte Erasmusbrücke längst zum Wahrzeichen für diesen Brü-
kenschlag und für Rotterdam insgesamt geworden.

held by its filigree components. Painted light blue the pylon and
cables seem connected to the sky. Even its heavy counter bearing
concrete base, ramps, and balustrades embody the movement of
dynamic form. A lifting bridge that can be opened for the passage of
ships forms its southern end; it is known to be the heaviest bascule
bridge in Western Europe.

Whether for its symbolism or elegance, the Erasmus Bridge dramatically lit at night, has become a symbol of bridging and of Rotterdam as a whole.

# KLAPPBRÜCKE UND BRÜCKENWÄRTERHAUS, PURMEREND (NL)
# BASCULE BRIDGE AND BRIDGEMASTER'S HOUSE, PURMEREND (NL)

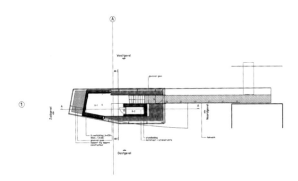

Die Tatsache zu vermitteln, dass Infrastruktureinrichtungen Teil der gestalteten Umwelt sind und entsprechender Aufmerksamkeit bedürfen, ist von alters her ein Anliegen der Architekten gewesen. Denn der einfachere Weg ist der ohne sie, wenn städtische Ämter und Fachingenieure sich einer Aufgabe mit möglichst wenig Aufwand entledigen, wobei sie die Architekten nur als Störfaktor wahrnehmen.

In Purmerend ist es den Architekten gelungen, mit den Ingenieuren auf Augenhöhe zusammenzuarbeiten. Zunächst galt es, die komplexen Zusammenhänge zwischen dem Kreuzungsverkehr zweier vielspuriger Straßen und dem zu überquerenden Kanal zu analysieren und danach die Kapazität der Klappbrücke zu dimensionieren. Die Architekten separierten die vier Fahrspuren von den Fußgänger- und Fahrradspuren und kamen so zu drei voneinander unabhängigen, wie Finger über den Kanal greifenden Brückendecks.

Das Haus des Brückenmeisters ist eine zeitgemäße Neuinterpretation des in Holland tausendfach in Versionen aus verschiedenen Jahrhunderten anzutreffenden Bautyps der Brückenwarte. Die Funktionsaufteilung ist immer gleich: technische Installationen im unteren Bereich, darüber ein möglichst hoher Standort mit Umsicht für den Brückenwärter, der die sich nähernden Schiffe schon von Weitem wahrnehmen muss, um den Verkehr zu disponieren.

Der Betonsockel findet seine Fortsetzung im Steg, der den Zugang zum Wärterhäuschen bildet, und verwächst mit dem Brückenkopf, nicht anders als beim Zollhäuschen einer mittelalterlichen Brücke.

UNStudio has always been concerned with conveying the fact that infrastructural installations belong to the designed environment; therefore, they require attention. It would be easier not to take that attitude. Architects are often regarded as a nuisance by city authorities and engineers who wish to perform their tasks with as little extra effort as possible.

In Purmerend, they were able to work as equal partners with the engineers. The architects' first task was to analyse the complex connections involved in intersecting traffic between two four-lane roads and the canal to be bridged. After that, the capacity and dimensions of the bascule bridge needed to be worked out. The four vehicle-lanes were separated from the pedestrian and cyclist lanes, creating three bridge decks; these are independent of each other and open like fingers above the canal.

The bridgemaster's house is a contemporary reworking of a building type that has been erected thousands of times throughout the Netherlands in versions from different centuries. The functional organisation is always the same; technical installations are on the lower level and a look-out position is as high above as possible. The upper level gives the bridgeman a panoramic view of his surroundings so that he can see ships approaching in the distance and control the traffic.

This building's concrete plinth extends to form a jetty, which provides a link to the bridgeman's house and merges with the bridgehead; just like the customs house of a medieval bridge. Rather

Die Warte selbst, mit ihrer Steckmetallfassade als technisches Bauwerk ausgewiesen, steht nicht im Lot, sondern neigt sich über das Wasser, als solle dadurch die Aufmerksamkeit des Brückenmeisters noch gesteigert werden. „Alles unter Kontrolle", signalisiert das Bauwerk. Die schrägen Wände verstärken die Dynamik, vermitteln den Eindruck von Bewegung: ein echtes Verkehrsbauwerk. Die perforierte Metallhaut, mal durchscheinend, abends hinterleuchtet, lässt das technische Innenleben des Gebäudes erahnen. Es handelt sich um *architecture parlante*, die von jedermann verstanden wird.

than remaining in line with the site, the control point, identifiable as a technical building by its extruded metal façade, leans over the water as if to heighten the bridgemaster's concentration. "Everything under control," is what the building seems to say. Its slanting walls underline the structure's dynamism, giving the impression of movement—a real traffic building. The perforated steel plate skin, through which light shines during the day and which is lit up from behind at night, provides a glimpse of the building's technical interior. This construction is an example of *architecture parlante*; it can be understood by all.

# WASSERVILLEN, ALMERE (NL)
# WATER VILLAS, ALMERE (NL)

Die Monotonie vorstädtischer Reihenhausbebauung sollte durchbrochen werden und die Siedlungshäuser für durchaus privilegiertes Wohnen am Wasser sollten einen individuelleren Lebensstil ermöglichen. Diese Ziele verfolgte die Verwaltung der jungen Stadt Almere (sie befindet sich auf neuem Land, das vor 40 Jahren noch vom IJsselmeer bedeckt war) und beauftragte mehrere Architekten mit entsprechenden Entwürfen.

Ben van Berkel entwickelte ein Prinzip variabel komponierbarer Betonkuben, die scheinbar frei und regellos zueinander stehen und deren Anordnung selbst bei Reihenhäusern zu einer abwechslungsreichen Bebauung führt. Die Grundeinheit eines Hauses besteht zunächst aus drei gestapelten, kastenförmigen Modulen mit den Abmessungen von zehn Meter Länge, sechs Meter Breite und drei Meter Höhe. Das obere ist jeweils in der Längsachse verschoben, wodurch einerseits ein überdachter Freibereich, andererseits ein Balkon entsteht. Außerdem bestand für die Klienten das Angebot, ihre Wohnfläche durch Zusatzmodule zu erweitern, leichte Stahlkonstruktionen, die an die Betonbauten angehängt werden konnten.

Während die Betonkuben mit Solidität ausstrahlenden anthrazitfarbenen Klinkern verkleidet sind, wurden die Zusatzmodule mit kupferfarbenen Metallpaneelen ummantelt, wodurch sich ein angenehmer Farbkontrast ergibt. Die Beschränkung auf wenige formale Mittel, die Verwendung von Farben und Materialien in ihrer strukturellen Vielfalt und die Vermeidung individuellen Wildwuchses waren die gestalterischen Zielsetzungen der Architekten.

28 der 48 Hauseinheiten sind an Stichstraßen in Reihen zusammengefasst und an der straßenabgewandten Seite von Wasser umgeben; 20 Einheiten stehen als Doppelhäuser an einer Gracht. Die Häuser bieten ein Maximum an Bezügen zum privaten Außenraum, zu den kommunikativen Erschließungsflächen und zum Wasser. Durch die variable Baukörperstruktur und den disziplinierten Einsatz weniger Materialien ergibt sich ein abwechslungsreiches Gesamtbild der aus 48 Hauseinheiten bestehenden Anlage, die dennoch Gelassenheit und eine gewisse Eleganz ausstrahlt und damit eine höherwertige Wohnqualität signalisiert.

The main idea here was to break up the monotony of suburban row housing estates, while leaving room for a more individual lifestyle at a privileged waterside residential location. This was the brief that came from the city of Almere when it commissioned designs from various architects. The new city is situated on reclaimed land that was still covered by Lake IJssel forty years ago.

Ben van Berkel developed a concept for cement modules that can be combined in various ways. They appear to have free and unregulated relationships to each other, which has created a multifaceted structure although these are actually row houses. The basic unit of each house consists of three stacked, box-like modules measuring 10 by 6 by 3 metres (length x width x height). Each upper level is extended in the longitudinal axis to create a covered terrace on one side and a balcony on the other. The clients could also extend their living spaces by adding extra modules of light steel to the concrete buildings.

While the concrete modules are clad in anthracite-coloured bricks that denote solidity, the additional modules are coated in copper-coloured metal panels, creating a pleasant colour contrast. The architects' design objectives were to use a limited range of formal methods, to exploit the structural variety of colours and materials, and to avoid incoherent individualistic elements.

Twenty-eight of the forty-eight housing units have been placed in rows around cul-de-sacs; they are surrounded by water on the side facing away from the street. Twenty further units have been built as semi-detached houses along a canal. The houses provide maximum connections to private outside space, communicative shared space and the water.

As a result of the varied structure and the disciplined use of only a few materials, the overall impression of this forty-eight-house development is lively. At the same time, it exudes calmness and a certain elegance, reflecting its high residential standard.

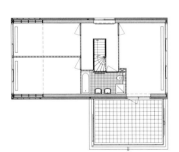

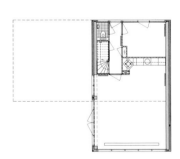

# MÖBIUS HAUS, HET GOOI (NL)
# MÖBIUS HOUSE, HET GOOI (NL)

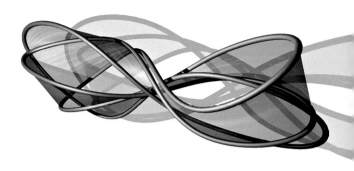

Fünf Jahre dauerte die Arbeit an dem ambitionierten Projekt eines Einfamilienhauses nahe Amsterdam. Dem Entwurf des skulpturalen Gebäudes liegt das Prinzip des Möbiusbandes zugrunde. Alle Räume sind schleifenförmig in Form einer liegenden Acht aneinandergereiht. So entpuppt sich das scheinbar labyrinthische Raumgeflecht auf zweieinhalb Geschossen als einfaches Erschließungssystem.

Der Zugang liegt unspektakulär an der Südseite. Wichtiger und häufiger frequentiert mag auf dem abgelegenen Waldgrundstück die Zufahrt in die Garage sein, die im Zentrum des Hauses liegt und direkten Zugang zum Vestibül hat. Von hier aus geht es einerseits über eine Rampe zum Wohnbereich, andererseits über eine Treppe zu einem der Studios. Die beiden Arbeitsbereiche der im Haus ihrem Beruf nachgehenden Ehepartner an den Enden des Gebäudes bilden die räumlichen Antipoden des Hauses. Wohnen, Schlafen und Kochen fügen sich an und vollenden die Endlosschleife. Als geschlossene Räume sind nur die Schlaf- und Gästezimmer und die Nasszellen ausgebildet, alle anderen Funktionen erfüllt ein das Haus durchziehendes Raumkontinuum, in dem die Raumsegmente in ihrer Nutzung wenig oder gar nicht vorbestimmt sind. Durchblicke und Ausblicke auf dem Rundgang sind auf vielfältigste Art inszeniert.

Die Ästhetik des Möbius-Hauses ist von wenigen Materialien und deren kontrastreicher Kombination geprägt: Sichtbeton, leicht grün getöntes Glas, Holzverschalungen an Decken und Parkett an wenigen, ausgewählten Partien. Massive Tische, Theken, Bänke

Work on this ambitious single-family home project near Amsterdam took five years to complete. The design of this sculptural building is based on the principle of the Möbius strip. All of its rooms have been positioned along a loop in the shape of a figure of eight. A seemingly labyrinthine network thus turns out to be a simple spatial system of communication.

The entranceway is located unspectacularly to the south. However, the access to the garage on this secluded forested site is probably more important and is frequented more often. It has been positioned at the centre of the house with a direct connection to the vestibule. From there a ramp leads on one side to the living area while a staircase on the other side goes up to one of the studios. Both of the spouses practice their professions within the house in two separate working areas, one at each end, which form the spatial antipodes of the building. Living areas, bedrooms, and kitchen area complete the infinite loop. Only the bedrooms, guest rooms, and bathrooms have been designed as closed spaces. All of the other functions are accommodated by the spatial continuum that pervades the building, the spatial segments of which have functionally been more, less, or not at all pre-defined. Views through the building and perspectives of the circuit have been orchestrated in the most diverse ways.

The aesthetics of this building are defined by the use of few materials and their contrasting combination; fair-faced concrete, glass tinted slightly green, wood-clad ceilings, and parquet flooring at a few chosen spots. Massive tables, counter tops and benches grow

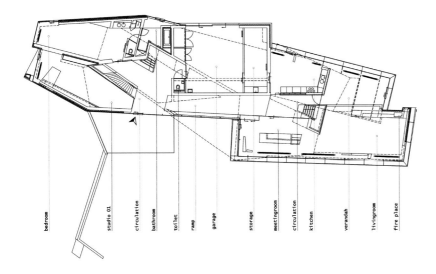

bedroom · studio 01 · circulation · bathroom · toilet · ramp · garage · storage · meetingroom · circulation · kitchen · verandah · livingroom · fire place

wachsen aus der Betonskulptur des Hauses heraus, die anderen Möbel sind konsequent als „Mobilien" aufgefasst und auf Rollen gestellt.

Wäre die Formenwelt nicht so expressionistisch, scharfkantig, schiefwinklig polygonal – der rechte Winkel erscheint fast nur in der Vertikalen – man wurde den Bau der aktuellen Strömung des Minimalismus zurechnen. Vielmehr gehört er jedoch dem Dynamismus an, denn er thematisiert die Raum-Zeit-Beziehung, die Dynamik des Raumes, die Bewegungsabläufe des täglichen Lebens.

from the concrete sculpture of the building. All other furnishings have been consistently designed as "movables" and been mounted onto wheels.

If the shapes that appear here were not so expressionistic, sharp-edged, oblique-angled polygonal—right angles are to be found only in the vertical direction—one would categorise the building within the current trends of Minimalism. However, it belongs much more to Dynamism as it addresses the space-time relationship, the dynamics of space and the courses of movement of everyday life.

# VILLA NM,
# UPSTATE NEW YORK
# (USA)

Das auf einem Hügel in der Nähe von Woodstock gelegene Wo-chenendhaus bricht mit den Traditionen des historischen Villenbaus, aber auch mit dem von Ludwig Mies van der Rohe und Walter Gro-pius vorgegebenen Idealtypus der aus Kuben arrangierten moder-nen Villa. Denn es verdankt seine Form nicht einer volumetrischen Komposition, sondern einem Torsionsvorgang. Eine langgestreckte Schuhschachtelform wurde vertikal zur Hälfte eingeschlitzt und ge-gabelt. Die beiden auf diese Weise entstandenen „Zinken" wurden jeweils um 90 Grad gedreht und gleichzeitig die eine ein halbes Geschoss nach unten, die andere nach oben gebogen, sodass sich zusammen mit dem unverändert gebliebenen Raumteil eine Split-Level-Situation ergab.

Durch die Drehung wurden Wände zu Boden und Decke und um-gekehrt. Der nach unten führende Körper schmiegt sich an den Hang, der obere erhebt sich über das Gelände und überdacht einen Stellplatz. Er wird von einer V-Stütze getragen. Das Haus demonstriert das von UNStudio postulierte „Inklusiv-Prinzip" der nahtlosen Verbindung heterogener Teile unter Ignorierung tekto-

This weekend house, located on a hill near Woodstock, breaks with the traditions of historical villa building, also moving away from the ideal modern cube-type villa as defined by Ludwig Mies van der Rohe and Walter Gropius. Its shape is born of a process of torsion rather than a volumetric composition. A stretched shoe box shape was vertically slit to its center and then forked. The two "prongs" that emerged were each rotated about an angle of 90 degrees and bent half a storey, one downwards and the other upwards, to create a split level situation in conjunction with the unaltered part.

The rotation led walls to become floors and ceilings and vice versa. The downward volume nestles against the slope while the upper one is raised above the plot to provide shelter to a parking spot; it is supported by a V-column. This building demonstrates the "Inclusive Principle" postulated by UNStudio of seamlessly connecting het erogeneous parts while neglecting tectonic principles and avoiding fractal methods. This artificial-appearing volume subtly unites with the surrounding nature through its dark brown color and its reflect ing panes of plate glass.

nischer Prinzipien und Vermeidung fraktaler Methoden. Durch die dunkelbraune Farbgebung und die den umgebenden Wald reflektierenden Spiegelglasscheiben vereint sich das künstlich erscheinende Artefakt auf subtile Weise mit der umgebenden Natur.

Im Inneren ist die monolithische Struktur des Gebäudes in reinweißer Körperlichkeit erlebbar. Von der im tiefen Bauteil liegenden Küche geht der Blick ein Halbgeschoss die Treppe hinauf ins Licht und zum raumhoch verglasten Wohnbereich mit weitschweifendem Ausblick. Nach einer Kehrtwendung führt eine ähnliche Treppe ein weiteres Halbgeschoss hinauf in den Schlafbereich mit zwei Schlafzimmern und einem Bad. Der Torsionsbereich des Raumes wird jeweils durch die schwebenden Treppen überbrückt. Auf diese Weise kommen Ruhe und Bewegung bei der Nutzung des Hauses im Charakter des Raumes zum Ausdruck.

Nach einem Brand im Jahr 2008 wird das Haus in etwas erweiterter Form neu aufgebaut.

The monolithic structure of the building can be experienced in pure white on its inside. A view extends from the kitchen, situated in the lower section of the house, half a storey up the stairs to a light floor-to-ceiling glazed living area with a rambling vista. Around a U-turn, a similar staircase leads a further half storey up to the sleeping area, which accommodates two bedrooms and a bathroom. The areas of torsion within the space are each bridged by a floating staircase. The calmness and movement that characterize the use of this house thus find spatial expression within it.

Following a fire in 2008, the building will be reconstructed in a slightly extended version.

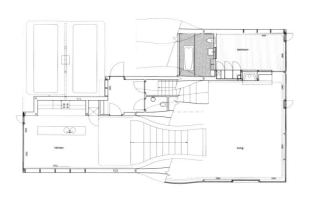

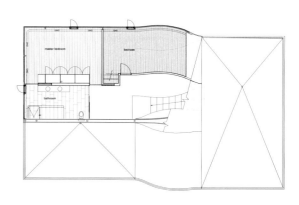

# THEATER AGORA, LELYSTAD (NL)

In Lelystad lässt sich das Scheitern der modernen Architektur be-
obachten. Das multifunktionale Zentrum musste nach einem Vier-
teljahrhundert wieder abgebrochen werden. Ein Neuanfang wird
gewagt, unter anderem mit dem neuen Theater „Agora", das als
Kristallisationskern für eine lebendige Stadtmitte dienen soll.

„You can't miss it", wird dem Besucher am Bahnhof der Weg ge-
wiesen, drüben der „feurige Diamant" ist es, wegen der kantigen,
kristallinen Form seiner Trapezblechfassade so genannt. Zu überse-
hen ist das ungewöhnliche, in roten, orange und gelben Farbtönen
signifikant gefärbte Bauwerk nicht. Doch zu verkennen auch nicht,
denn im Unterschied zu zahlreichen neuen Theaterbauten zeigt es
die seit Gottfried Semper archetypische Form eines Theaters mit
Eingangsfront, breiterem Zuschauerhaus und schmalem Bühnenturm, wenn auch grob in Aluminium gefaltet und geschnitten. Die
Architekten griffen zu den radikalen formalen Mitteln, um der depri-
mierenden Mediokrität des Ortes einen Leuchtturm entgegenzu-
setzen. Der Theaterbesuch soll etwas Besonderes sein, schon das
Gebäude soll ein intensives Raumerlebnis bieten, voller Emotionali-
tät und Verve, und so setzt sich die Farbensinfonie im Inneren fort,
hier mit kräftigen Pink- und Rottönen.

Viel Platz für eine großzügige Halle stand auf dem knappen Grundstück nicht zur Verfügung und so entwickelt sich das Foyer räumlich
in die Höhe, windet sich geradezu um den Saal und bietet eine Viel-
zahl von Aufenthalts- und Sitzmöglichkeiten für den Pausenplausch,
aber auch ein eindrückliches Architekturerlebnis. Die pinkfarbenen
Treppenläufe schießen kreuz und quer durch den Raum und geben
ihm etwas Dramatisches; die Farborgie wird zusätzlich befeuert,
wenn Tageslicht durch das große Oberlicht hereinflutet.

Im nach der Sponsorfirma benannten „Scarletzaal" glühen Sitze
und Wände in tiefem Theaterrot. Das Motiv der Facettierung des Au-
ßenbaus taucht hier wieder als Wandgestaltung auf und entwickelt
segensreiche akustische Eigenschaften. Es gibt keine Ränge, nur

The failure of modern architecture can be witnessed in Lelystad.
Its multifunctional town centre had to be abandoned after nearly a
quarter of a century of work. A new beginning has now been initi-
ated; the new "Agora" Theater will form the core of its lively town
center.

"You can't miss it", is what the enquiring visitor is told upon arrival
to the station, it's that "fiery diamond" over there, so called for
the angular, crystal-like shape of its corrugated façade. There is no
way to overlook this unusual eye-catching building, clad in tones
of red, orange and yellow. It is also impossible to mistake it for
anything other than a theatre. In contrast to many new theatres,
this one demonstrates the archetypical shapes that have been ac-
cepted in theatre building since Gottfried Semper. It is comprised of
an entrance façade, a wide auditorium, and a narrow stage tower,
albeit roughly folded and cut in aluminium. The architects applied
radical formal means to counteract the depressing mediocrity of
this location through a beacon project. A visit to the theatre should
be something special; the building itself should provide an exciting,
intense emotional experience. Thus, the symphony of color applied
to the outside extends in the same spirit into the inside in strong
pink and red tones.

There was not enough room on the small site for a generously sized
entrance hall, so the foyer spatially evolves upwards, winding itself
around the auditorium and providing opportunity to, sit and chat
during the breaks; an impressive architectural experience. Pink balustrades shoot every which way through the space, giving it a dra-
matic feel; a color effect that is fired on by daylight falling through
the large skylight.

The seats and walls of the auditorium, called "Scarletzaal" after the
sponsor, glow in deep theatre red. The facetted effect of the outside
façade reappears in the wall design here, where it demonstrates
good acoustic qualities. This auditorium is not tiered although it

einen Balkon als zweite Ebene der Zuschauersitze. Die 715 Plätze sind unter Verzicht auf einen Mittelgang so nah wie möglich an die Bühne gerückt. Die Dichte hat Auswirkung auf die ungewöhnlich intime Atmosphäre und die Akustik des Saals. Die renommierten Akustikplaner von DGMR Arnheim haben sich um den Klangraum gekümmert und offenbar hervorragende Bedingungen geschaffen.

Der kleine „Van Wijnenzaal" mit 207 (quittegelben) Plätzen und ausfahrbarer Tribüne hat Blackbox-Charakter und ist multifunktional nutzbar, als Studiotheater oder für Konferenzen und Festlichkeiten. Das Publikum erlebt in seinem neuen Agora-Theater Aufführungen aller Sparten, die als fertige Produktionen angeliefert werden, aber auch Rockmusik, Shows und Musicals. Die Bühne mit 500 Quadratmetern ist groß genug für das Bolschoi-Ballett, doch Neben- und Hinterbühnen sowie Stauraum für Produktionen gibt es nicht, man arbeitet „just-in-time" aus dem LKW.

Wie im modernen Theaterbau üblich, sind die internen Diensträume in der Ausstattung von ausgesuchter Kargheit, mit Ausnahme des Mitarbeiterfoyers, das wie ein edles Café wirkt. Es ist vornehm dunkel getäfelt und liegt an prominenter Stelle direkt über dem Haupteingang.

In wenigen Städten kann das Theater aufgrund seiner architektonischen Erscheinung eine derartige Bedeutung im Stadtbild beanspruchen. Das neue Stadthaus und die Einkaufspassage können dagegen nicht ankommen. Für die Besucher und die reisenden Akteure bietet das Agora-Theater prägende Eindrücke. Kein schlechter Zug für ein Provinztheater, dem überregionale Aufmerksamkeit üblicherweise nicht zuteil wird.

does have a second level of seats on the balcony. Its 715 seats have been positioned as close to the stage as possible without a central aisle. The density adds to its unusually intimate atmosphere and the acoustics of the space. The sound environment was engineered by renowned acoustic planners von DGMR Arnhem, who have obviously managed to achieve excellent results.

The smaller "Van Wijnenzaal" auditorium with 207 (quince yellow) seats and an extendable tribune is of black box character; it is multifunctional and can be used for studio theatre, conferences or festivities.

Audiences of the new Agora Theater are given the opportunity to view a variety of performances including rock concerts, shows, and musicals. Its 500-square-metre stage is large enough to accommodate the Bolschoi Ballet, however there was no space leftover for secondary spaces and back stage; lack of storage space means that everything must be carried onstage directly from the back of the trucks.

As is common in modern theatre building, the internal service rooms are decidedly austere in composition with the exception of the staff foyer, which has the air of a noble café. It is mainly dark panelled and is prominently positioned above the main entrance.

Only in few towns does the architectural appearance of a theatre lead it to take on such a significant role within an urban context. The new town hall and shopping mall have little chance beside it, as the Agora Theater leaves a lasting impression on visitors and travelling actors alike. Not a bad position for a regional theatre, which would not usually receive so much national attention, to find itself in.

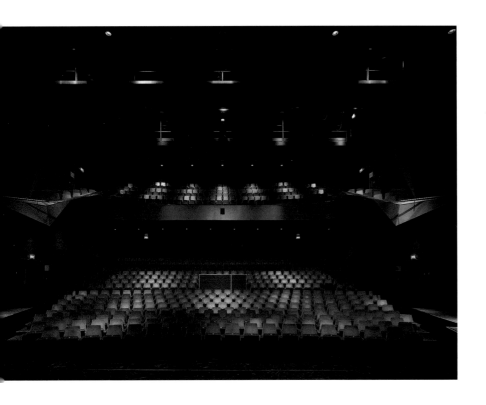

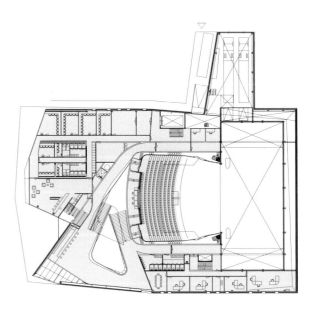

# KARBOUW VERWALTUNGSGEBÄUDE, AMERSFOORT (NL)
## KARBOUW OFFICE, AMERSFOORT (NL)

© Jan Derwig

© Jan Derwig

Das Werkstatt- und Verwaltungsgebäude einer Bauunternehmung gehört an seinem Standort in einem Gewerbegebiet eher zu den bescheideneren Anwesen. Wenn es dennoch ins Auge fällt, so zum einen durch seine Materialität: die Klinkerfassade des massiveren Erdgeschosses und die Metallfassade des aus Stahl konstruierten Obergeschosses aus Trapezblechen, die ungewöhnlicherweise mit horizontal verlaufenden Stegen montiert wurden. Ein weiterer gestalterischer Kunstgriff hebt den Bau aus seiner Umgebung heraus: der zunächst unmotiviert erscheinende Knick und die halbseitige Verschiebung des Obergeschosses.

Der Knick bewirkt eine Dynamisierung des Baukörpers und des Innenraums. Er hat jedoch auch den Effekt, dass die kühn vorkragende Glasfront des Bürotrakts aus der allgemeinen Gebäudeflucht der Straße tritt und sich dem Ankömmling zuwendet, der sich von der Zubringerstraße her nähert. Eine Bewegung hin zum Besucher, eine Willkommensgeste also, die der ebenfalls vortretende gläser-

This workshop and administration building, which belongs to a construction company, is one of the more modest structures in its industrial park location. Nevertheless, it features eye-catching elements, one of which is its materiality. The façade of the massive ground floor is made of brick, while the metal façade of the steel-structured top floor is made of corrugated sheeting, which has unconventionally been mounted horizontally. A further artistic move, which also distinguishes the building from its surroundings, is an initially unmotivated-seeming bend and a half-sided shift in the upper storey.

The bend lends dynamism to the building volume and the interior space. However, it also produces the effect that the boldly cantilevering glass front of the office section projects out of line with the buildings in the street, turning towards visitors to the building who approach it via an access road. This represents a movement towards the visitor, a welcoming gesture, underlined by an equally

© Jan Derwig

ne Eingangsturm an der Ecke wiederholt. Das Haus zeigt Gesicht und Charakter und hebt sich dadurch von den teilweise weit voluminöseren, aber gesichtslosen Nachbarbauten ab.

Der Eingang mit anschließender Treppe führt zu den Büros im Obergeschoss, die durch die leicht gewölbte Decke ein eigenes räumliches Gepräge erhalten. Schon der Empfangstresen mit seiner schwungvollen, fraktal gebrochenen Figur stimmt auf die Raumeindrücke ein, die von gekippten Fassaden und schrägen Türgewänden wie von bewegten Kräften bestimmt sind. Die sorgfältige Detaillierung und die eigens entworfenen und gebauten Einbaumöbel und Schreibtische zeigen einen für derlei Gewerbebauten ungewohnten Standard und runden den Gesamteindruck ab.

Gemeinsam mit dem Umspannwerk in Amersfoort steht Karbouw am Beginn einer Reihe von Bauten, deren Entwürfe von *mobile forces* geformt scheinen, wie sie im weiteren Werk von UNStudio immer stärkeren Einfluss gewannen.

protruding glazed entrance tower on the corner. This building demonstrates character and boldness, distinguishing itself from the much more voluminous yet bland neighbouring structures.

The entrance and an adjoining staircase lead to an office on the upper floor, which is characterised by a slightly curving ceiling. A reception desk, with a sweeping, fractured form, leads the way for the spatial experience to come; defined by tilted façades and movable walls that appear to have been formed by dynamic forces. Careful detailing along with self-designed and built furnishing units and desks demonstrate an unusually high standard in industrial building.

Along with the transformer station in Amersfoort, Karbouw belongs to a series of buildings whose designs were shaped by the "mobile forces" theme, which has become increasingly significant within the work of UNStudio.

# BÜROZENTRUM LA DEFENSE, ALMERE (NL)
# LA DEFENSE OFFICES, ALMERE (NL)

Einen Steinwurf nördlich des Bahnhofs, am Übergang zu den reinen Wohngebieten, markiert das Bauvorhaben den Rand der City und des Gebiets höherer Dichte und Bebauung im Zentrum der jungen Stadt Almere. Von größerer Flächenausdehnung als die Nachbarbebauung, bildet das Bürozentrum mit den beiden mehrfach geknickten und ineinander greifenden Baukörpern einen eigenen, umgrenzten Campus, dessen Innenhof auf der Ebene +1 liegt, also von den Randstraßen aus über Rampen zugänglich ist. Der Komplex steigt als Ganzes in seiner Bauhöhe kontinuierlich von vier auf sieben Geschosse an und vermittelt damit zwischen der niedrigeren Bebauung im Norden und der höheren City im Süden.

Das Thema von Innen und Außen wird besonders mit den Fassaden durchgespielt, die technisch und konzeptionell zunächst nichts Außergewöhnliches an sich haben. Prinzipiell handelt es sich um horizontal gegliederte, umlaufende Bandfassaden mit wenig Variabilität, die mit ihrer Gleichförmigkeit den ganzen Komplex zusammenfassen. Ihr Erscheinungsbild wird jedoch wesentlich durch die Farbigkeit geprägt. Während sich die äußeren Fassaden in einem unspektakulären Aluminium-Grau gegen die Umgebung eher abweisend zeigen, leuchtet es flammend aus den Höfen heraus, in den buntesten Farben.

Verantwortlich für den irisierenden Effekt der Hoffassaden ist eine spezielle Hinterglasfolie, die hier erstmals im Bauwesen Verwendung fand. Die Folie reflektiert das Licht in der Art eines Prismas in den verschiedensten Farben und unterschiedlich, abhängig von der Position des Betrachters, vom Winkel, von der Besonnung oder von der abendlichen Hinterleuchtung. Auf diese Weise ändert sich die Atmosphäre im Innenhof ständig.

Der Innenhof, in den Verlauf innerstädtischer Wegebeziehungen eingebunden, wird, obwohl privaten Ursprungs, zur städtischen Attraktion. Das großflächige Bürozentrum, obwohl hermetisch angelegt, öffnet sich und wird in das urbane Netzwerk der Stadt eingebunden.

Located a stone's throw away from the train station and bordering on purely residential areas, this building project marks the edge of town; an area of higher population and construction density at the centre of the new city of Almere. The dimensions of the office complex are larger than those of its neighbouring buildings. Its two volumes, which fold several times and are intertwined with one another, form their own defined campus. There is an inner courtyard on the +1 level that is accessible from the surrounding streets by ramps. The whole complex rises in height from four to seven storeys, reflecting the lower buildings in the north and the higher buildings in the south of the city.

The relationship between interior and exterior is primarily expressed through the building's façades, which initially appear to be quite usual in technical and conceptual terms. They are composed of bands of windows arranged horizontally around the buildings without much variety; their uniformity is representative of the entire complex. However, their appearance is defined to a large extent by their colour. While the external façades are almost standoffish towards their surroundings in an inconspicuous aluminium-grey, dazzling light emerges from the courtyard in the brightest of colours.

The courtyard façades' iridescent effect is created by a special plastic film on the inside of the windows that was used here for the first time ever in construction. The film reflects light in a type of prism and in many different colours, which vary according to the location of the observer, the angle, the sunlight or the evening backlight. As a result, the atmosphere in the courtyard changes constantly.

The courtyard, which is linked to inner-city pedestrian routes, has become a sightseeing attraction, despite being originally planned as a private space. Although the large office complex is laid out hermetically, it opens up and connects with the urban network of the city.

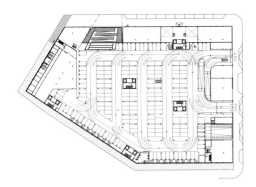

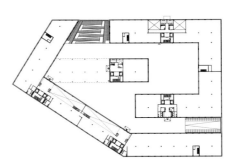

# KAUFHAUS GALLERIA, SEOUL (KR)
# GALLERIA DEPARTMENT STORE, SEOUL (KR)

„Luxuriöser, aber trotzdem trendy und einzigartig", sollte das Modewarenhaus durch die Umgestaltung werden. Im exklusiven Einkaufsviertel Apgujeong-dong gelegen, soll es sich schon durch sein Äußeres gegen die starke Konkurrenz behaupten. Die Architekten entwarfen eine „lebendige" Fassade, die ihr Aussehen ständig wandelt. Sie besteht aus 4330 runden Scheiben aus sandgestrahltem, laminiertem Glas, in das eine irisierende Folie eingelassen ist. Dadurch reflektieren und brechen die Scheiben das einfallende Licht je nach Betrachtungswinkel und sorgen tagsüber für ein abwechslungsreiches Erscheinungsbild in allen Farben des Regenbogens.

Die Nachtbeleuchtung durch LEDs lässt sich für jede Scheibe per Computer nach Farbe und Helligkeit individuell steuern, wodurch sich unendliche künstlerische und thematische Gestaltungsmöglichkeiten ergeben. Andere Programme scheinen dem Chamäleon abgeschaut, spiegeln Ereignisse, Moden, Jahreszeiten wider oder sind Ausdruck künstlerischer Ideen. Da die Scheiben eine starke Eigenwirkung haben, handelt es sich nicht um eine herkömmliche Bildschirmfassade, sondern das Haus behält allzeit seine wiedererkennbare Eigencharakteristik.

Im Inneren leiten „Laufstege" die Kunden durch die allgemeinen Verkaufsflächen und von einem individuell gestalteten Markenladen zum nächsten. Die catwalks werden durch entsprechende Leuchtdecken begleitet und bringen Licht, Bewegung und gleichzeitig Übersicht und Orientierung in das Haus. Auch die vertikalen Räume mit den Rolltreppen sind mit speziellen Gläsern verkleidet, die, teilweise mit Folien versehen, teilweise hinterleuchtet, mit einer komplexen, veränderbaren Lichtregie bespielt werden. Das Gebäude mit seiner wandelbaren Fassade und dem exklusiven Innenleben soll auf seine Art den ständig wechselnden Moden, die im Inneren dargeboten werden, den angemessenen Hintergrund bieten.

The brief was to redesign this clothing department store to make it "more luxurious, yet still trendy and unique." Located in the prestigious shopping area of Apgujeong-dong, the idea was that the building's exterior should assert itself in the face of strong competition. The architects designed a "lively" façade that constantly changes in appearance. It consists of 4,330 discs made of sandblasted, laminated glass, which each contain an iridescent foil. The film makes the discs reflect and break up light in accordance with the angle of vision, thus creating a changing image in all colours of the rainbow during the day. Light is produced by LED panels at night. The colours and brightness of each panel can be individually set by computer, providing never-ending artistic and design options. One related theme is the projection of weather conditions onto the façade. Other programmes appear to be modelled on the chameleon—they reflect events, fashion, and the seasons or they express artistic ideas. The impression of an ordinary computer screen façade is avoided as the discs have a strong impact of their own. The building always retains its own recognisable unique character.

Inside, "catwalks" lead clients through the general shopping areas, as well as from one individually designed brand name shop to the next. These catwalks are accompanied by ceiling illumination; they bring light and movement to the building as well as providing an overview and orientation. Vertical escalator spaces are clad in special types of glass. Some are covered in foils, while others are backlit and programmed with complex and modifiable lighting.

With its alterable façade and exclusive interior, the concept is that the building, in its own way, provides the appropriate background for the constantly changing fashions presented inside.

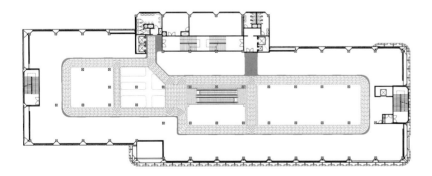

# PARK UND RIJN TOWERS, ARNHEIM (NL)
# PARK AND RIJN TOWERS, ARNHEM (NL)

Die beiden Hochhäuser am Arnheimer Hauptbahnhof sind die weithin sichtbaren Zeichen für die Umwälzungen, die am zentralen Verkehrsknotenpunkt der Stadt im Gang sind. 1996 begann die Masterplanung durch UNStudio für die *Transfer Zone Arnhem Central*. Ziel war, die chaotische, durch Provisorien sowie architektonischen und verkehrstechnischen Wildwuchs gekennzeichnete Situation vor dem Bahnhof zu ordnen und aufzuwerten. UNStudio bediente sich der diagrammatischen Entwurfsmethode, durch die alle statischen, dynamischen, ökonomischen und virtuellen Parameter zusammengeführt werden, um zu einer integrativen Lösung des komplexen Problems zu gelangen. Alle Verkehrsarten wie Eisenbahn, Busse, Taxis, PKW und Fahrräder wurden miteinander funktional und räumlich in engen Bezug gesetzt, um die Transfervorgänge der täglich 65.000 Reisenden zu optimieren. Wichtigstes Erkenntnisfeld für den Entwurf waren die Fußgängerbewegungsstudien. Eine in dynamischen Formen ausgebildete Transferhalle bildet den geschützten Raum für die Verkehrsströme und deren Verknüpfungen. Ein Geschäftszentrum mit Läden und Restaurants lagert sich an, bildet und nutzt Synergien gleichermaßen. Zu den bereits realisierten und von UNStudio konzipierten und gestalteten Bauteilen gehören ein Autotunnel, der Busbahnhof und die Tiefgarage. Dabei kamen von UNStudio und Ove Arup & Partners entwickelte „V-Collectors" zum Einsatz, V-förmige Stützeinheiten, die sich nach oben öffnen und Licht und Frischluft bis in die tiefste Terminal- und Garagenebene hinableiten.

Zwei Hochhäuser, Park und Rijn Towers genannt, dominieren als Tor zur Stadt das Bild des neuen Verkehrszentrums und tragen mit ihrem wirtschaftlichen Potenzial zur Funktion der *Transfer Zone* bei. Mit ihrer schlanken Form, die noch durch die dynamische Giebelausbildung betont wird, machen sie Bewegung und Verkehr zum

Two high-rise buildings at Arnhem Central Station are the most visible symbols of the changes taking place at the city's main transport node. UNStudio began the master planning of *Arnhem Centra Transfer Zone* in 1996. Its objective was to tidy up and upgrade the chaotic situation around the station, characterised by uncontrolled architectural and infrastructural growth. UNStudio applied a diagrammatic design method to the project, through which al statistical, dynamic, economic and virtual parameters could be combined to find an integrative solution to the complex problems involved. All modes of transport including trains, buses, taxis, cars, and bicycles were placed in functional and spatial relation to one another in order to optimise the daily transfer processes of up to 65,000 commuters. Pedestrian movement studies comprised the most important area of research within this design. A transfer hall, dynamic in form, provides sheltered space for the streams of transport and their intersections. A mall containing shops and restaurants merges with, creates, and exploits the synergies there. The building volumes conceived and designed by UNStudio that have already been constructed include a tunnel for car traffic, a bus station and an underground car park. V-shaped "V-Collector" columns developed by UNStudio and Ove Arup & Partners were used in the construction; they open up towards the top, allowing light and fresh air to enter right down to the deepest terminal and car park levels. Two high-rise buildings known as the Park and Rijn Towers visually dominate the new transport centre as a gateway to the city, adding with their economic potential to the success of the *Transfer Zone* Their slender shapes, which are emphasised by the dynamic form of their gables, express movement and transport. Balancing on a narrow plinth along the rail tracks, the lower levels cantilever diagonally to lift the buildings above the tracks.

gestalterischen Thema. Auf schmalem Sockel entlang der Bahngleise balancierend, kragen die unteren Geschosse schräg aus und heben den Hauskörper über die Gleise.

Horizontale Fensterbänder sind den beiden 18-geschossigen Hochhäusern gemeinsam. Die Fassade des Park Tower ist sowohl in der Tiefe durch hervortretende Fensterrahmen als auch in der Fläche durch abwechselnde Fensterhöhen und -längen gegliedert und zeigt ein grünes Farbspiel der Brüstungsfelder. Der Rijn Tower hingegen ist in sich vertikal in zwei Körper gegliedert und ansonsten mit einer glatten, silbern schimmernden Karosserie windschnittig verkleidet. Die Fensterbänder sind auf der Südseite aus Sonnenschutzgründen schmal, verbreitern sich an den abgerundeten Giebelseiten kontinuierlich und erreichen ihre größte Höhe an der Nordseite.

Mit zwei gänzlich verschiedenen Gestaltungsansätzen treten die beiden Hochhäuser also vor Augen, mit der Individualisierung der Kompartimente das eine und mit gesamtheitlicher Plastizität das andere, und doch sind sie Brüder.

Both of the eighteen-storey high-rises are characterised by horizontal bands of windows. The façade of the Park Tower is structured in depth by jutting out window frames and over the whole surface by alternating window heights and lengths, demonstrating a green play of colour in the balustrade panels. The Rijn Tower in contrast has been structured into two volumes and clad in streamlined smooth, silver, shimmery bodywork. Its bands of windows are narrow on the southern side for sun protection, gradually broadening out around the rounded gable sides to reach their maximum height on the northern side.

These two high-rises have thus been created using completely different design approaches—one with individualised compartments and the other with overall plasticity—yet their relation to each other remains very present.

# STAR PLACE, KAOHSIUNG (TW)

Die junge, expandierende Industriestadt Kaohsiung im Südwesten Taiwans mit Sonderwirtschaftszone, Werften und großem Containerhafen sucht noch nach ihrer Identität im ostasiatischen Wirtschaftsraum. Im Rahmen des anstehenden Strukturwandels wird das Zentrum der Stadt nach dem SHE-Konzept (*safe, healthy, ecological*) umgestaltet und aufgewertet. Die Stadt soll attraktiv, lebenswert und somit anziehend und konkurrenzfähig gemacht werden.

Dazu gehören auch Aufenthalts- und Einkaufsmöglichkeiten im gehobenen Sektor wie das neue, luxuriöse Einkaufszentrum Star Place. Als UNStudio in das Projekt eintrat, waren die Grundzüge des Gebäudes durch Dynasty Design Corp und HCF Architects aus Taipei bereits festgelegt. Insbesondere Form und Konstruktion des zwölfgeschossigen Baukörpers existierten bereits, sodass für UN-Studio typische Elemente wie stützenfreie Flächen nicht mehr realisiert werden konnten.

Das Grundstück liegt an einem Stadtplatz mit Kreisverkehr. Das Gebäude nimmt die Bewegung des Stadtraumes auf und reagiert mit seiner konkaven Form auf die städtebauliche Situation. Eine runde Kante vermittelt an der Schmalseite zum benachbarten Warenhaus, mit dem das Star Place über eine zweigeschossige, elegante Brücke verbunden ist.

Die Fassade zum Platz hin setzt die städtebauliche Bewegung fort und leitet sie in die Vertikale um. Thema der gläsernen Fassade ist ein signifikanter Moiré-Effekt, der nicht wie normalerweise erst in der Wahrnehmung durch die Überlagerung zweier Raster entsteht, sondern als dekoratives Element in fest gebauter Form existiert. Dazu ist die Fassade durch horizontale, auskragende Aluminiumlamellen und vertikale Glasschwerter in Rasterfelder mit Fensteröffnungen von gewisser Tiefe gegliedert, deren Breite variiert, wo-

The young, expanding industrial city of Kaohsiung in southwest Taiwan, complete with special economic zone, dockyards, and large container port, is still searching for its own identity within the East Asian economic area. Its centre is being reorganised and upgraded in line with the SHE (*safe, healthy, ecological*) concept, within the context of ongoing structural transformation. The main objective is to improve the city's attractiveness and quality of life, to make it more appealing, and therefore more competitive.

Part of that plan is to establish high-class leisure and shopping facilities such as the new luxurious Star Place shopping plaza. When UNStudio became involved in the project, its basic characteristics had already been defined by Dynasty Design Corp and HCF Architects from Taipei. The form and structure of the twelve-storey building volume had been erected so that UNStudio-typical features such as column-free spaces could no longer be incorporated.

The building is located at a city square on a traffic roundabout. It absorbs the urban motion around it, reacting to the spatial situation through its concave form. A rounded edge on its narrow side forms a transition to a neighbouring department store with which the Star Place is connected via an elegant two-storey bridge.

Its façade towards the square carries forward the surrounding urban movement, redirecting it in the vertical direction. The motif of this glazed façade is the Moiré effect. It is a decorative element in built form rather than, as is usually the case, emerging as the result of two overlapping patterns. The façade has been structured using horizontal, cantilevering aluminium lamellas and vertical fins of glass with window openings of significant depth and of varying width, to produce the overall effect, which is underlined at night by coloured, alternating LED lighting. The attractive appearance of this

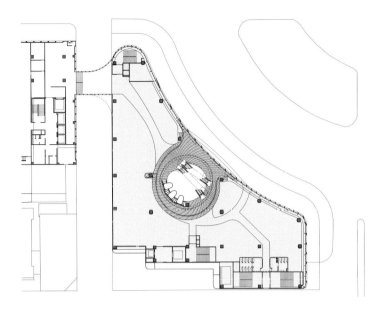

durch sich der großflächige Effekt ergibt. Verstärkt wird die Wirkung am Abend durch farbig wechselnde LED-Beleuchtung. Die attraktive nächtliche Erscheinung ist in China mit seiner Tradition der Nachtmärkte von besonderer Bedeutung.

Die Mitte des Gebäudes wird von einem Atrium eingenommen, das die Geschosse optisch und funktional zueinander in Bezug setzt und in dem drei Panoramaaufzüge auf und ab gleiten. Die Rolltreppen sind je Geschoss um zehn Grad versetzt, wodurch sich eine 110-Grad-Bewegung vom Erd- bis zum Dachgeschoss ergibt. Um das Atrium herum fließt ein offener Raum, von dem aus die einzelnen Läden des Shop-in-Shop-Kaufhauses zugänglich sind. Zwei bis sieben Einheiten können je Geschoss individuell eingerichtet werden. Das Atrium ist ihr vertikales Schaufenster.

Ziel der Gestaltung war, helle, transparente, frisch und modern wirkende Verhältnisse zu schaffen und die einzelnen Läden mit möglichst viel Außenbezug auszustatten. Bis zum zwölften Geschoss hinauf öffnet sich das Luxuskaufhaus zur Stadt hin und empfiehlt sich mit seinen Brand Shops zum Besuch. Das Haus ist Werbeikone und ein neues Wahrzeichen für die Stadt.

structure at night is of particular significance in the context of the Chinese tradition of night markets.

An atrium occupies the centre of the building, visually and functionally linking various levels to one another; three panorama-view elevators glide up and down. The escalators have been shifted by 10 degrees per level, thus producing a 110-degree movement from ground to top level. An open space flows around the atrium from which individual retail outlets within this shop-in-shop mall can be accessed. Two to seven units can be installed on each level, the atrium forming their vertical shop front.

The design aimed to establish a light, transparent, fresh, modern looking spatial situation and to provide each of the stores with maximum contact to the outside. This luxury shopping mall opens up to its topmost twelfth storey to the city, inviting a visit to one of its brand shops. It has become an icon of advertising and a symbol of the city.

# HOTEL & HAMAM, CASTELL, ZUOZ (CH)

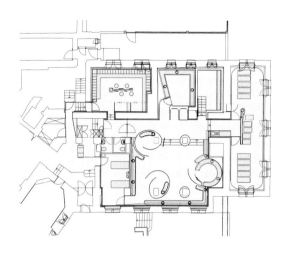

Das 1913 erbaute Kurhaus in Zuoz gehörte nach dem Ersten Welt-krieg als Hotel Castell zu den mondänsten Herbergen des Engadin. Nach dem langsamen Niedergang mit mehreren Besitzerwechseln und jahrelangem Leerstand sollte das Hotel 2006 zu einer neuen Blüte als Künstlertreffpunkt geführt werden. Um den Umbau zu finanzieren, errichtete der Bauherr neben dem Altbau ein luxuriöses fünfgeschossiges Apartmenthaus und ließ die 17 bis zu 300 Qua-dratmeter großen Eigentumswohnungen der „Chesa Chastlatsch" veräußern.

Das elegante Gebäude folgt mit einem Knick den Höhenlinien des Grundstücks. An der nach St. Moritz ausgerichteten Südseite öff-net sich das Haus ganzflächig mit Balkons am Westflügel und mit verglasten Veranden am Ostflügel. Die Grundrisse der Wohnungen wurden individuell unterteilt und eingerichtet. Über eine Verbindung mit dem Altbau können dessen Einrichtungen von den Bewohnern mit genutzt werden.

Im Hotel selbst hat UNStudio die Hälfte der Zimmer neu einge-richtet, nicht historisierend, nicht designorientiert, sondern eher sachlich, doch mit bewusst eingesetzten, dezenten Material- und Farbwirkungen. In der Beletage wurde das traditionelle Stuck- und Messing-Interieur beibehalten.

This spa hotel in Zuoz, built in 1913, was considered one of the most glamorous in the Engadin valley after the First World War; it was called the Hotel Castell. After its gradual demise following many changes of ownership and years of vacancy, the hotel was again to be injected with creative flair. The client erected a luxurious five-storey apartment building beside it in order to finance its con-version. Seventeen condominiums of up to three hundred square metres in the "Chesa Chastlatsch" building were put on the mar-ket.

A kink in this elegant building follows the contour lines of the site. Its southern side, which is oriented towards St. Moritz, completely opens up, with balconies on the west wing and glazed verandas on the east. The ground plans of the apartments were partitioned and arranged individually. A connection to the old building allows its inhabitants to access the hotel facilities.

UNStudio rather soberly remodelled half of the rooms in the actual hotel, neither in a historicising nor design-oriented manner yet with deliberately applied, understated material and colour combinations. The traditional stucco and brass interior of the belle étage was pre-served.

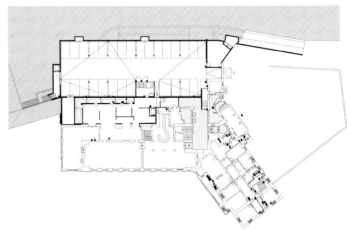

Attraktion des Hauses ist neben der „Roten Bar" von Pipilotti Rist das türkische Dampfbad im Tiefparterre. Van Berkel hat den traditionellen Hamam, den zentralen Kuppelraum mit peripheren Anwendungsräumen, neu interpretiert. Der zentrale Hauptraum ist in glühend rote und violette Farben getaucht. Die zylindrischen Glaswände der Reinigungsräume leuchten in unwirklichem Licht. Es gibt einen Kräuterdampfraum, einen Eukalyptusraum und ein „Goldbad" mit goldenem Glasmosaikbecken und schwarzen Schieferwänden. Der Hamam mit seiner intensiven Farblichtstimmung ist auf Verzauberung aus. 1001 Nacht ist allerdings kein Thema, denn jeglicher Anklang an den Orient wird vermieden.

A Turkish steam bath on the basement floor is a particular attraction within the hotel, as is the "Red Bar" by Pipilotti Rist. Van Berkel reinterpreted the traditional hamam, the central domed space and peripheral secondary rooms. A central main space has been doused in fiery red and purple tones. The cylindrical glazed walls of the cleansing rooms glow in surreal light. There is a herbal steam room, a eucalyptus room and a "golden bath" with golden miniature-tiled pool and black walls of slate. The hamam and its intense coloured-light atmosphere is enchanting, however, without an inkling of "1001 Nights"; any echoes of the orient have been omitted.

# JÜDISCH-HISTORISCHES MUSEUM, AMSTERDAM (NL)
# JEWISH HISTORICAL MUSEUM, AMSTERDAM (NL)

Sanierung und Umbau denkmalgeschützter Bauten gehört nicht zu den Alltagsaufgaben von UNStudio. Beim Jüdisch-Historischen Museum ging es um ein Ensemble aus vier ehemaligen Synagogen aus dem 17. und 18. Jahrhundert, die zu einem Museum zusammengefasst werden sollten. Dabei sollten die Funktionen und die Charakteristika der einzelnen Bauten erhalten bleiben. Die zwei größeren Gebäude werden als Synagoge und als Ausstellungs- und Depotgebäude genutzt. Die beiden schmaleren Häuser nehmen Foyer und Nebenräume auf, ergänzt um ein eingeschossiges Verbindungsbauwerk.

Die fließenden Räume des Foyer- und Erschließungsbereichs mit beschwingteren Formen stehen gegen die solideren Strukturen der barocken Baukörper. Unter der Neuen Synagoge wurde ein Untergeschoss eingebaut, um Platz für einen klimatisierten Ausstellungsraum und für ein Auditorium zu schaffen.

Vorherrschende und die Bauteile unterschiedlicher Epochen verbindende Farbe ist Weiß. Kräftige Farbakzente, hier ein gelber Raum, da ein purpurfarbenes Treppenhaus, dort eine grün hinterleuchtete, gelochte Wand, akzentuieren die modernen Bauteile. Stühle von Arne Jacobsen in Kombination mit Tischen und Einbaumöbeln von UNStudio und das helle Licht bringen eine heitere Atmosphäre mit sich, wie man sie beim äußeren Anblick der vornehmen barocken Backsteinarchitektur nicht erwarten würde.

Restoring and converting listed buildings is not one of UNStudio's everyday tasks. The Jewish Historical Museum project involved an ensemble of four former synagogues dating back to the seventeenth and eighteenth centuries. They were to be amalgamated to form one museum, leaving the functions and characters of each of the buildings intact. The two larger ones are used as synagogues and exhibition and depot buildings, while the two narrower structures accommodate the foyer and secondary spaces. A single-storey building acts as a connecting volume.

Flowing foyer and communication spaces are curvaceous in contrast to the more solid baroque building volumes. A basement floor was constructed under the new synagogue to provide room for air-conditioned exhibition areas and an auditorium.

The colour white dominates, associating various building parts from different eras to one another. Modern elements are accentuated by a yellow room here, a purple staircase there, a green rear-lit perforated wall somewhere else. Chairs by Arne Jacobsen in combination with tables and built-in furniture by UNStudio and bright light create a cheerful atmosphere that comes unexpectedly inside such noble baroque redbrick architecture.

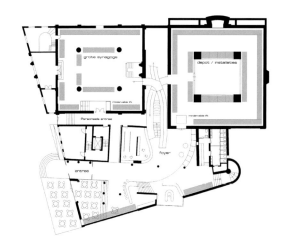

# FORSCHUNGSLABOR, GRONINGEN (NL)
# RESEARCH LABORATORY, GRONINGEN (NL)

Ein Laborgebäude für mikrobiologische Forschung hat keinen Besucherverkehr und wird nur von wenigen Forschern genutzt. Es ist hochtechnisch ausgestattet und hat keine Beziehungen nach draußen. Deshalb besitzt das Gebäude keine Fenster. Da es jedoch in einem von Fußgängern stark frequentierten Quartier steht, haben ihm die Architekten eine attraktive Fassade verliehen, die eine Art Transparenz zumindest andeutet. Die vertikalen, schmalen Aluminiumpaneele drehen sich an manchen Stellen wellenförmig nach außen und scheinen ein farbiges Innenleben dem Straßenraum zuzuwenden. Mit steigender Höhe von gelb nach grün wechselnd, wird der umgebende Garten reflektiert.

Die Fassade des Hauses findet sich im Inneren, denn es wird durch zwei Lichthöfe belichtet, einen, der sich nach oben konisch verjüngt, einen, der sich nach oben weitet. Wendeltreppen sorgen für die innere Verbindung der Geschosse. Das Gebäude ist in vier mikrobiologisch-hygienische Sicherheitsstufen unterteilt. Über der Versorgung im Erdgeschoss sind Räume der Verwaltung untergebracht. Darüber liegt ein Technikgeschoss zur Konditionierung der Laborräume im 3. und 4. Obergeschoss. Im Dachgeschoss ist wiederum Haustechnik untergebracht. Der Haupteingang zu den Labors befindet sich im 4. Obergeschoss (intern Level 2), von wo aus eine Brückenverbindung zum benachbarten WMF-Gebäude besteht.

In den Labors richten sich die vorherrschenden Farben nach den technischen Anforderungen. In den zentralen Erschließungszonen bringen kräftige Farben von einem hellen Gelb auf der untersten, am wenigsten belichteten Ebene über Orange bis zu einem kräftigen Rot im obersten Geschoss eine freundliche Stimmung ins Haus und entschädigen für die Tatsache, dass man nicht die Umgebung, nur den Himmel über den Glasdächern zu sehen bekommt.

A laboratory for microbiological research does not have regular visitors and is only used by a few researchers. As it is equipped with high-tech instruments and has no relationship with the outside world, the building does not have any windows. However, it is located in an area used by many pedestrians, so the architects have given it an attractive façade that at least hints at a type of transparency. At some points its narrow vertical aluminium panels turn outwards in a wave-like movement, appearing to reveal to the street a coloured interior. Their gradually increasing height and change of colour from yellow to green reflect the surrounding garden.

The building's façade is located inside as it receives its light through skylights above two interior courtyards, one of which tapers upwards conically, while the other opens out as it rises. Spiral staircases connect the floors to one another. The building is divided into four microbiological-hygienic levels of security. The administration rooms are located on the first storey, above the maintenance department floor. On the second floor, a technical level provides conditioning for the laboratories on the third and fourth floors. A building services department is located on the top floor. The main entrance to the laboratory is on the fourth floor (internal level 2), from which a bridge connects to the neighbouring WMF building. The dominant colours used in the laboratories are based on technical requirements. In the central laboratory space, strong colours ranging from light yellow at the lowest level, which receives the least natural light, to orange in the middle levels, and finally to an intense red on the top floor, create a friendly atmosphere. They compensate for the fact that there are no views of the surrounding area and that the sky can only be seen through a glass roof.

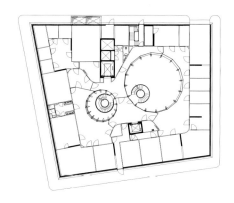

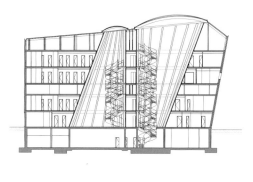

# INTERIEUR UND DESIGN
# INTERIOR AND DESIGN

Wenngleich Produktdesign an Architekturschulen kaum gelehrt wird, hat das Metier die Architekten zu allen Zeiten magisch angezogen. Nicht erst seit Bruno Paul, Le Corbusier oder Mies van der Rohe ist es Usus, dass namhafte Architekten ihren Stuhl, ihre Liege oder gar ihr Möbelprogramm entworfen. Peter Behrens hatte von der Leuchte bis zum Briefkopf alles entworfen, was in den Anfängen der Moderne der neuen Form bedurfte. Ben van Berkel befindet sich also sowohl in guter Tradition als auch in bester Gesellschaft, wenn seine Designs in den Katalogen der einschlägigen Firmen auftauchen, die Möbel bei Knoll neben der Arbeit von Kollegen wie Eisenman, Gehry, Hollein oder Venturi, das Geschirr bei Alessi neben Chipperfield, Hadid, Rashid oder Zumthor.

Zunächst und später immer wieder ging es um Interieurs, um Ausstellungsarchitektur, um Pavillons, um „Kleinarchitektur", die im Entstehungsprozess von weitaus weniger Einflussfaktoren bestimmt und von reduzierter Komplexität ist. Fingerübungen sozusagen, um die Formfindung zu trainieren. Zu der endgültigen Form, so scheint es, haben diese Übungen bei UNStudio noch nicht geführt, auch nicht zu einer entschiedenen Formensprache. *Blob* oder *box*, die Entscheidung ist noch nicht gefallen. Wird die *Summer-of-Love*-Ausstellung in der Frankfurter Schirn 2005 in von

Although product design is not often taught at schools of architecture, it has fascinated architects of all eras. Bruno Paul, Le Corbusier or Mies van der Rohe were not the first renowned architects to design a chair, sofa or even an entire range of furniture. Peter Behrens designed everything—from lamps to letterheads—which required a new design in the early days of the modern era. Therefore, Ben van Berkel is both in good company and part of a long tradition when his work appears in the catalogues of various firms. His furniture designs for Knoll are pictured alongside work by colleagues such as Eisenman, Gehry, Hollein, or Venturi, and his tableware for Alessi is beside that created by Chipperfield, Hadid, Rashid, or Zumthor.

Van Berkel's earlier work included interiors, exhibition designs, pavilions, and "small architecture," which are subject to far fewer internal and external factors and are less complex than large-scale architecture. He later continued to work in those fields. One could describe them as finger exercises, which he used to find his own form. It appears that these exercises at UNStudio have not yet led either to a final form or to a fixed language of form. Blob or box— the choice has not yet been made. The *Summer of Love* exhibition at the Schirn Kunsthalle in Frankfurt in 2005 was presented in spaces shaped by broad bands that snuggled up to the walls and

AUSSTELLUNG *SUMMER OF LOVE*, KUNSTHALLE SCHIRN FRANKFURT AM MAIN 2005 *SUMMER OF LOVE* EXHIBITION, KUNSTHALLE SCHIRN FRANKFURT AM MAIN 2005 INSTALLATION *THE CHANGING ROOM*, ARCHITEKTURBIENNALE VENEDIG 2008 *THE CHANGING ROOM* INSTALLATION, VENICE BIENNALE OF ARCHITECTURE, 2008

breiten Bändern geformten Räumen präsentiert, die sich an die vorhandenen Wände schmiegen und sanft kurvend ihre Richtung ändern, gibt sich die Rauminstallation in der Ausstellung *Holiday Home 2006* im Institute for Contemporary Art Philadelphia, USA hart und kantig und lebt vom Kontrast des weißen, kristallinen Körpers, aus dessen Innerem es glühend rot leuchtet wie aus einer Rubindruse. Wer in dieses *Holiday Home* eintritt, erfährt durch die fraktalen Raumkompartimente und die fast schmerzhaft intensive Farbe ein ungekanntes, betörendes Raumerlebnis.

Die Architektur-Biennale 2008 in Venedig beschickte UNStudio mit der Installation *Changing Room*. Der zwischen den Säulen der Corderia im Arsenale aufgestellte Pavillon entwickelte seine Form aus sich ständig wandelnden und drehenden Flächen, die mal die Wand, mal den Boden, mal die Decke bildeten. Unterstützt durch Projektionen und Lichteffekte, beeinflusste das verwirrende Raumerlebnis die Befindlichkeit der Besucher und warf die Frage auf, wie sich die künftigen, in hohem Maß ortlosen und unvorhersehbaren Arbeits- und Lebensverhältnisse auf die architektonische Umwelt auswirken werden.

Einem solchen „inklusiven" Raum entspricht vielleicht das von der holländischen Firma Gispen anlässlich der Ausstellung *Living*

changed direction in gentle curves. In contrast, the spatial installation for the *Holiday Home 2006* exhibition at the Institute for Contemporary Art in Philadelphia, USA, was hard and angular. It was vitalised by the contrast between its white, crystalline body and its interior, which projected a glowing red light like a ruby geode. These fractal compartments and almost painfully intense colour gave visitors to the *Holiday Home* exhibition a strange and beguiling spatial experience.

UNStudio enlivened the Venice Architecture Biennale 2008 with their *Changing Room* installation. The shape of the pavilion, located between the pillars of the Corderia dell'Arsenale, evolved from constantly changing and turning areas that sometimes formed walls and at other times floor or ceiling. This confusing spatial experience was made more complex by projections and lighting effects. The changing room also altered visitors' sensitivities. Its aim was to pose the question of how future, and to a large extent dislocated and unpredictable working and living conditions, would affect the architectural environment.

That sort of "inclusive" room can be compared to the special office furniture called *Sum Workplace* designed for the Dutch firm, Gispen, for the *Living Tomorrow* exhibition in 2004. The furniture allows

*Tomorrow* 2004 herausgebrachte sonderbare Büromöbel *Sum Workplace*, das dem Benutzer die Entscheidung offen lässt, wie er arbeiten möchte, ob im Kauern, im Sitzen, im Stehen, oder eben das Möbel raumgreifend umrundend und abwechselnd die Tischblätter in verschiedenen Höhenlagen benutzend. Poliertes Gussaluminium und Edelholzplatten sorgen für eine kostbare Anmutung, als handle es sich um übergroßes Silbergeschirr.

Reales Tafelsilber hatte UNStudio schon 2001 für die Firma Alessi für deren Serie von Tee- und Kaffeeservices berühmter Designer entwickelt. Selbstverständlich wurde diese Aufgabe nicht durch raffiniertes Gestalten mehr oder weniger eleganter, mehr oder weniger praktischer Kännchen und Tassen gelöst. Ein *design model* kam wieder zum Einsatz, ein mathematisches Modell. Die „Klein'sche Flasche", benannt nach dem Mathematiker Felix Klein, die als dreidimensionales Pendant zum Möbiusband ins Blickfeld Ben van Berkels geriet. Es handelt sich um einen Schlauch, der in sich selbst gestülpt eine endlose Fläche ergibt, die gleichzeitig innen und außen ist. Aus diesem Element mit kontinuierlicher Oberfläche entstanden die ovalen Teile des Services. Das zugehörige, wie ein wehendes Seidentuch geformte Tablett mit den Mulden für das

the user to decide how he or she would like to work—crouching, standing, sitting, or in any other position by relocating the table components at various heights and positions in space. Polished cast aluminium and precious wood panels exude luxury, resembling over-sized silverware. UNStudio had already designed real silverware in 2001 for Alessi's series of tea and coffee sets by famous designers. They naturally did not approach the task by sophisticatedly designing more or less elegant, or more or less practical pots and cups. A design model was again used—a mathematical model. This time it was the Klein Bottle, named after the mathematician Felix Klein, which caught Ben van Berkel's eye as a three-dimensional counterpart to the Möbius strip. It involves a tube pieced together to produce an infinite space that is simultaneously outside and inside. With its continuous outer surface, this element provided the impetus for the oval pieces of the set designed by van Berkel. The matching tray, shaped like a blowing silk scarf, has troughs for the cups and saucers and may be used on both its silver and honey-coloured coated-plastic sides.

A more conventional tray was designed for Alessi in 2004. The round *Switch Tray* has the surprising feature that it can be used

SILBERTABLETT *SWITCH TRAY*, ALESSI 2005 *SWITCH TRAY* SILVER TRAY, ALESSI 2005 ARBEITSPLATZ *SUM*, GISPEN 2005 *SUM* WORKPLACE, GISPEN 2005

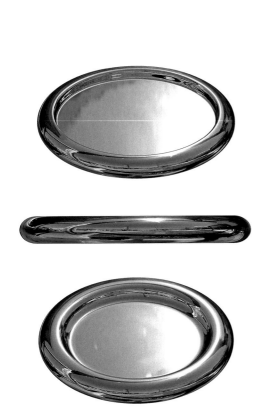

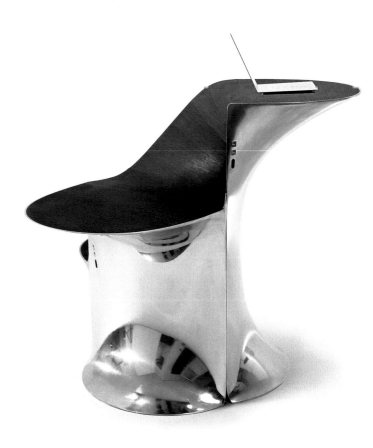

Geschirr lässt sich von der silbernen wie von der mit honiggelbem Kunststoff beschichteten Seite benutzen.

Ein eher konventionell erscheinendes Tablett wurde 2004 für Alessi entwickelt. Das kreisrunde *Switch Tray* hat jedoch eine überraschende Eigenschaft. Auch dieses lässt sich umdrehen und anders benutzen (also *switchen*, umschalten). Eine Seite ist für Lebensmittel gedacht, sie hat einen sanft ansteigenden Rand, der die Entnahme beispielsweise von Nüssen oder Konfekt erleichtert. Die andere Seite ist für Flaschen und Gläser besser geeignet, weil sie einen steilen Rand aufweist, an dem die Gläser anstoßen, aber nicht aufrutschen können.

2005 machte sich Ben van Berkel an die Arbeit, für die Firma Knoll ein Sofa zu entwerfen. Sein Interesse für sich wandelnde Morphologien konzentrierte sich auf die Kontur von Polstermöbeln. So ließ er die Querschnittsform eines Sessels kontinuierlich in jene einer Liege übergehen. Und weil dies in einer kreisförmigen Bewegung geschieht, bekam das Möbel den Namen *Sofa Circle*. An einem Ende kann man bequem sitzen, am anderen eher liegen, und dazwischen macht man es sich gemütlich, wie es gerade genehm ist. Das halbkreisförmige Möbel gibt es auch im Negativ, wodurch

for different functions on both sides. One side is for food and has a gently rising edge, making it easier to serve items such as nuts or confectionary. The other side is more suitable for bottles and glasses as it has a steep edge that the glasses can lean against without falling off the tray.

In 2005, Ben van Berkel began working on the design of a sofa for Knoll. He applied his fascination for changing morphologies to the contours of upholstered furniture, allowing the cross-section of an armchair to mutate into a couch. As this occurs in a circling movement, the furniture was called *Circle Sofa*. One can sit comfortably at one end, while the other end is better suited to lying down; the middle section is more flexible in function. The semi-circular furniture is also available in reverse form. It can be expanded to create a snake-like, room-filling, potentially endless row, or completed to form a circle. Rather than merely being an object, this furniture shapes the surrounding space.

When Ben van Berkel was commissioned to design a chair for Knoll in 2008, he realised that architects take a very different approach to designing chairs than furniture designers. The architect starts with the space and surroundings, in which the chair will become a part.

SITZMÖBELSYSTEM *SOFA CIRCLE*, WALTER KNOLL INTERNATIONAL 2005 *SOFA CIRCLE* SEATING SYSTEM, WALTER KNOLL INTERNATIONAL 2005

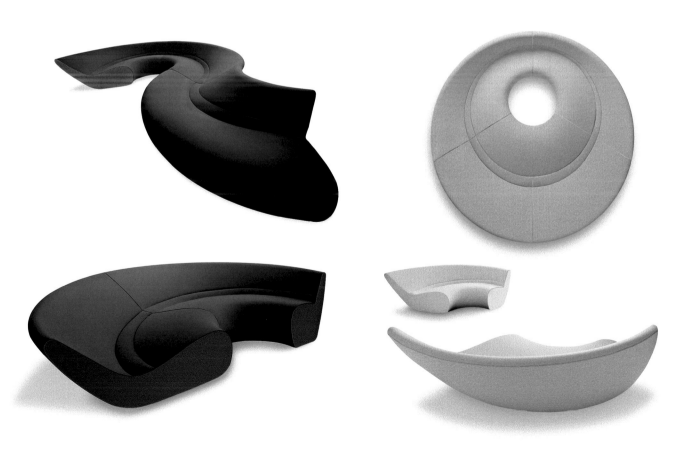

MYCHAIR, WALTER KNOLL INTERNATIONAL 2008 *MYCHAIR*, WALTER KNOLL INTERNATIONAL 2008 *DER LÄNGSTE TISCH DER WELT FÜR ALLE KULTUREN*, IMM MÖBELMESSE KÖLN 2008 *THE WORLD'S LONGEST TABLE FOR ALL CULTURES*, IMM COLOGNE FURNITURE FAIR 2008 © Roland Borgi

es sich zu einer schlangenförmigen, raumgreifenden, potenziell endlosen Reihe vervielfältigen oder zu einem Kreis komplettieren lässt. Das Möbel ist nicht nur Objekt, sondern gestaltet den es umfließenden Raum.

Dass der Architekt sich einer Aufgabe wie der Gestaltung eines Sitzmöbels ganz anders annimmt als ein Möbeldesigner, ist Ben van Berkel 2008 klar geworden, als er im Auftrag der Firma Knoll einen Stuhl entwerfen sollte. Der Architekt fängt mit dem Raum und der Umgebung an, von dem der Stuhl ein Teil sein wird. Alle Eigenschaften des Stuhls werden auf ihre räumlichen Effekte hin untersucht. Das räumliche Objekt ist in der Lage, je nach Betrachtungswinkel andere Ansichten zu zeigen. *After image* nennt van Berkel das Prinzip der unterschiedlichen Eindrücke, die sich aus Spiegelungen und Echos ergeben, wenn Formen und Schwünge des Metallrahmens sich aus verschiedenen Blickwinkeln und im gepolsterten Teil wiederholen. Hinzu kommen die verschiedenen Sitzpositionen, die der Stuhl zulässt, ja anbietet, die den Benutzer zur häufigen Änderung seiner Haltung animieren und damit zur Änderung von Ansichten und Perspektiven. So kann sich jeder den Stuhl zu eigen machen, deshalb der Name *MYchair*.

All of the features of the chair are examined from the perspective of their effects on the space. Spatial objects can make different impressions depending on the position from which they are viewed. Van Berkel calls the principle of multiple impressions *after image*. It results from the reflections and echoes created as the shapes and curves of the metal frame are repeated from different angles and in the upholstered part of the chair. The chair also allows—indeed, provides—different sitting positions, encouraging the user to alter his or her position, thus causing a change of view and perspective. Everyone can make the chair his or her own, which is why it is called *MYchair*.

In 2008, van Berkel also designed the "longest table for all cultures" for the IMM (International Furnishing Show) in Cologne, Germany. Its modular design means that the table can be expanded by adding different elements to make it as long as is required. Its components reflect home situations such as a Sunday brunch, a snatched breakfast, a late night snack, housework and so on. The multiple identities and functions of the table also represent van Berkel's view of international audiences, the "strongest common factor" in the hustle and bustle of a trade fair.

© Roland Borgmann

*DER LÄNGSTE TISCH DER WELT FÜR ALLE KULTUREN*, IMM MÖBELMESSE KÖLN 2008 *THE WORLD'S LONGEST TABLE FOR ALL CULTURES*, IMM COLOGNE FURNITURE FAIR 2008

Ebenfalls 2008 entwarf van Berkel den „längsten Tisch für alle Kulturen" eigens für die Möbelmesse in Köln. Modular aufgebaut, kann er um verschiedene Elemente bereichert und auch beliebig verlängert werden. Die Elemente thematisieren häusliche Situationen wie den Sonntagsbrunch, das hastige Frühstück, den *late night snack*, die Hausarbeit usw. Die multiple Identität und Multifunktionalität ist aber auch van Berkels Kommentar auf das internationale Publikum, den „stärksten gemeinsamen Faktor" des quirligen Messetrubels.

Möbel und Produktdesign sind für den Architekten eine besondere Herausforderung, weil er sich eigentlich auf ein fremdes Terrain begibt. Andererseits reizen ihn die Gestaltungsmöglichkeiten mit wesentlich weniger Parametern, als er normalerweise zu bedenken hat. Wenngleich er es offenbar nicht lassen kann, den Prozess durch Anwendung seiner gewohnten Entwurfsmethoden, funktionalen und philosophischen Überlegungen zu bereichern. So stecken in den Designobjekten auch viele Reflexionen aus der Gedankenwelt des Architekten, und das macht ihren Reiz aus.

Furniture and product design pose a particular challenge to architects as they involve working in unfamiliar territory. However, architects are attracted by the opportunity to design using far fewer parameters than must normally be taken into account. Architects seem unable to refrain from enriching this field with the use of their familiar design methods and their functional and philosophical thinking. As a result, such designed objects reveal many thoughts from an architect's mind, which makes them so intriguing.

# PROJEKTBETEILIGTE
# PROJECT CREDITS

**"MUMUTH", Graz:** Ben van Berkel, Caroline Bos with Hannes Pfau and Miklos Deri, Kirsten Hollmann, Markus Berger, Florian Pischetsrieder, Uli Horner, Albert Gnodde, Peter Trummer, Maarten van Tuijl, Matthew Johnston, Mike Green, Monica Pacheco, Ger Gijzen, Wouter de Jonge
**Engineering:** Arup London

**Het Valkhof Museum, Nijmegen:** Ben van Berkel with Henri Snel, Remco Bruggink, Rob Hootsmans, Hugo Beschoor Plug, Walther Kloet, Marc Dijkman, Jacco van Wengerden, Luc Veeger, Florian Fischer, Carsten Kiselowsky
**Interior:** Ben van Berkel, Remco Bruggink

**Mercedes-Benz Museum, Stuttgart:** Ben van Berkel, Caroline Bos with Tobias Wallisser and Marco Hemmerling, Hannes Pfau, Wouter de Jonge, Arjan Dingsté, Götz Peter Feldmann, Björn Rimner, Sebastian Schaeffer, Andreas Bogenschütz, Uli Horner, Ivonne Schickler, Dennis Ruarus, Erwin Horstmanshof, Derrick Diporedjo, Nanang Santoso, Robert Brixner, Alexander Jung, Matthew Johnston, Rombout Loman, Arjan van der Bliek, Fabian Evers, Nuno Almeida, Ger Gijzen, Tjago Nunes, Boudewijn Rosman, Ergian Alberg, Gregor Kahlau, Mike Herud, Thomas Klein, Simon Streit, Taehoon Oh, Jenny Weiss, Philipp Dury, Carin Lamm, Anna Carlquist, Jan Debelius, Daniel Kalani, Evert Klinkenberg
**Realization:** UNStudio/ Wenzel + Wenzel, Stuttgart
**Engineering:** Werner Sobek Ingenieure, Stuttgart

**Tea House on Bunker, Vreeland:** Ben van Berkel, Gerard Loozekoot with René Wysk, Job Mouwen and Marcel Buis, Thomas de Vries, Holger Hoffmann, Eric den Eerzamen, Joakim Kaminsky, Peter Irmscher, Daniel Kalani, Anika Voigt, Eric Coppolse, Stephan Albrecht
**Engineering and construction:** ABT, Velp

**NMR Facility, Utrecht:** Ben van Berkel with Harm Wassink, Ludo Grooteman, Walter Kloet, Mark Westerhuis, Jacco van Wengerden, Aad Krom, Paul Vriend, Marion Regitko, Jeroen Kreijnen, Henri Snel, Laura Negrini, Remco Bruggink, Marc Prins

**Prince Claus Bridge, Utrecht:** Ben van Berkel with Freek Loos, Ger Gijzen and Armin Hess, Suzanne Boyer, Jeroen, Jacques van Wijk, Ludo Grooteman, Henk Bultstra, Tobias Wallisser, Ron Roos
**Engineering foundations:** DHV, Amersfoort
**Engineering pylon and deck:** Halcrow UK, London and Swindon

**Erasmus Bridge, Rotterdam:** Ben van Berkel with Freek Loos, Hans Cromjongh, Ger Gijzen, Willemijn Lofvers, Sibo de Man, Gerard Nijenhuis, Manon Patinama, John Rebel, Ernst van Rijn, Hugo Schuurman, Caspar Smeets, Paul Toornend, Jan Willem Walraad, Dick Wetzels, Karel Vollers

**Bascule Bridge and Bridgemaster's House, Purmerend:** Ben van Berkel with Freek Loos, Ger Gijzen and Sibo de Man, John Rebel, Stefan Böwer, Stefan Lungmuss
**Management and engineering advisors:** IBA, Amsterdam

**Water Villas, Almere:** Ben van Berkel with Gianni Cito, Henri Snel, Boudewijn Rosman, Alex Jung, Katrin Meyer, Aad Krom, Andreas Bogenschütz, Yuri Werner, KSK Tamura, Jasper Jägers, Stella Vesselinova, Martin Kuitert

**Möbius House, Het Gooi:** Ben van Berkel with Aad Krom, Jen Alkema, Matthias Blass, Remco Bruggink, Marc Dijkman, Casper le Fevre, Rob Hootsmans, Tycho Soffree, Giovanni Tedesco, Harm Wassink

**VilLA NM, Upstate New York:** Ben van Berkel with Olaf Gipser and Andrew Benn, Colette Parras, Jacco van Wengerden, Maria Eugenia Diaz, Jan Debelius, Martin Kuitert, Pablo Rica, Olga Vazquez-Ruano
**Project consultant:** Roemer Pierik, Rotterdam

**Theater Agora, Lelystad:** Ben van Berkel, Gerard Loozekoot with Jacques van Wijk, Job Mouwen and Holger Hoffmann, Khoi Tran, Christian Veddeler, Christian Bergmann, Sabine Habicht, Ramon Hernandez, Ron Roos, Rene Wysk, Claudia Dorner, Markus Berger, Markus Jacobi, Ken Okonkwo, Jorgen Grahl-Madsen **Executive architect:** B+M, Den Haag

**Karbouw Office, Amersfoort:** Ben van Berkel with Aad Krom Kasper Aussems, Frank Verhoeven, Stephan de Bever
**Engineering:** Buro Bouwpartners, Hilversum

**La Defense Offices, Almere:** Ben van Berkel with Marco Hemmerling, Martin Kuitert, Henri Snel, Gianni Cito, Olaf Gisper, Yuri Werner, Marco van Helden, Eric Kauffman, Katrin Meyer, Tanja Koch, Igor Kebel, Marcel Buis, Ron Roos, Boudewijn Rosman, Stella Vesselinova

**Galleria Department Store, Seoul:** Ben van Berkel and Caroline Bos with Astrid Piber, Ger Gijzen, Cristina Bolis, Markus Hudert, Colette Parras, Arjan van der Bliek, Christian Veddeler, Albert Gnodde, Richard Crofts, Barry Munster, Mafalda Botelho, Elke Uitz, Harm Wassink
**Structural engineers:** Arup & Partners (Schematic Design)
**Lighting design:** Arup Lighting

**Park and Rijn Towers, Arnhem:** Ben van Berkel, Gerard Loozekoot with Henri Snel, Olaf Gipser, Tobias Wallisser and Ton van den Berg, Jacco van Wengerden

**Star Place, Kaohsiung:** Ben van Berkel, Caroline Bos, Astrid Piber with Ger Gijzen, Christian Veddeler, Mirko Bergmann, Albert Gnodde, Sebastian Schott, Freddy Koelemeijer, Katja Groeger, Jirka Bars, Andreas Brink, Simon Kortemeier, Shu Yan Chan
**Executive architects:** HCF Architects, Planners & Associates, Taipei
**Lighting design:** UNStudio, ArupLighting, Amsterdam
**Façade animation content:** UNStudio, Lightlife, Cologne, Alliance Optotek Corporation, Hsinchu, Taiwan

**Hotel and Hamam, Castell, Zuoz:** Ben van Berkel with Olaf Gipser and Pablo Rica, Sebastian Schaeffer, Andrew Benn, Dag Thies, Eric den Eerzamen, Ron Roos, Claudia Dorner, Martin Kuitert, Marco Hemmerling, Sophie Valla, Tina Bayerl, Peter Irmscher
**Executive architect:** Walter Dietsche AG, Chur

**Jewish Historical Museum, Amsterdam:** Ben van Berkel, Harm Wassink with Arjan van der Bliek and Derrick Diporedjo, Khoi Tran, Colette Parras

**Research Laboratory, Groningen:** Ben van Berkel, Gerard Loozekoot with René Wysk, Erwin Horstmanshof and Jacques van Wijk, Wouter de Jonge, Eric den Eerzamen, Nanang Santoso, Ton van den Berg, Boudewijn Rosman, Thomas de Vries, Michaela Tomaselli, Andreas Bogenschuetz, Pablo Rica, Jeroen Tacx, Eugenia Zimmermann, Stephan Albrecht, Anika Voigt **Construction:** ABT, Velp

## Ben van Berkel

Prof. Ben van Berkel, geboren 1957 in Utrecht, arbeitete zunächst als Grafikdesigner, während er an der Rietveld Akademie in Amsterdam Architektur studierte. 1982 ging er an die Londoner Architectural Association und diplomierte dort 1987. Er arbeitete in den Büros von Zaha Hadid in London und Santiago Calatrava in Zürich. 1988 wurde Van Berkel & Bos Architectuurbureau gegründet. 1999 wurde das Büro durch Hinzuziehung weiterer Spezialisten auf eine breitere Basis gestellt und in UNStudio umbenannt.

Nach Gastprofessuren an der Columbia University in New York, an der Harvard University, der Princeton University, dem Berlage Institut Rotterdam und an der UCLA Los Angeles leitet er seit 2001 die Architekturklasse der Städelschule in Frankfurt am Main. Zu den zahlreichen Preisen und Ehrungen gehört auch die Auszeichnung für UNStudio als „Architekt des Jahres 2007" des ArchitectenWerk.

Professor Ben van Berkel was born in Utrecht in 1957. He worked as a graphic designer while studying architecture at the Rietveld Academy in Amsterdam. In 1982, he moved to the Architectural Association in London and graduated in 1987. He worked in the offices of Zaha Hadid in London and Santiago Calatrava in Zurich. The Van Berkel & Bos architectural practice was founded in Amsterdam in 1988. It was renamed UNStudio in 1998 after being expanded to incorporate further specialists.

Following positions as a visiting professor at Columbia University in New York, Harvard University, Princeton University, the Berlage Institute in Rotterdam, and UCLA, Ben van Berkel has been the Dean of the Architecture Class at Städel Art Academy in Frankfurt since 2001. Among his many prizes and awards, Ben van Berkel was named "Architect of the Year 2007" by ArchitectenWerk.

## Caroline Bos

Caroline Bos, geboren 1959 in Rotterdam, studierte Kunstgeschichte am Birkbeck College der University of London. In dieser Zeit entstanden in Zusammenarbeit mit Ben van Berkel zahlreiche Artikel für die niederländische Zeitung *De Volkskrant*. Wenige Jahre nach Gründung des Büros Van Berkel & Bos beendete sie ihre Tätigkeit als Journalistin und widmete sich der internen Arbeit, um alles Schriftliche, vom Anstellungsvertrag über Projektbeschreibungen bis hin zu Essays und Veröffentlichungen, zu übernehmen und jegliche Projekte des Büros als interne Kritikerin zu begleiten.

Gemeinsam mit Ben van Berkel gab sie die im Büro entstandenen Bücher heraus, darunter *Delinquent Visionaries* (1993), *Mobile Forces* (1994), *Move* (1999), *Unfold* (2002) und *Design Models* (2006).

Sie lehrte an der Princeton University, dem Berlage Institut Rotterdam, an der UCLA Los Angeles und an der Academie van Bouwkunst in Arnheim.

Caroline Bos was born in Rotterdam in 1959 and studied art history at Birkbeck College, University of London. During that time, she and Ben van Berkel wrote many articles for the Dutch newspaper, *De Volkskrant*. She stopped working as a journalist a few years after the foundation of Van Berkel & Bos in order to devote herself full-time to the practice and to take care of all written tasks there. These ranged from employment contracts and project descriptions to essays and publications. She also accompanied all of the practice's projects as an internal critic.

Caroline Bos and Ben van Berkel have co-written several books about the work of their practice, including *Delinquent Visionaries* (1993), *Mobile Forces* (1994), *Move* (1999), *Unfold* (2002) and *Design Models* (2006).

Caroline Bos has taught at Princeton University, the Berlage Institute in Rotterdam, UCLA and the Academy of Architecture in Arnhem.

Harm Wassink
Partner = Senior Architect

Astrid Piber
Partner = Senior Architect

Gerard Loozekoot
Partner = Senior Architect

## SECHZEHN FRAGEN
## SIXTEEN QUESTIONS

**Falk Jaeger** Gibt es Lehrer in Ihrer Ausbildung, durch die Sie besonders geprägt wurden?
**Ben van Berkel** Keine einzelne Person, eher Gruppen, die mich jeweils in einzelnen Aspekten meiner Arbeit beeinflusst haben. Ich hatte nie ein Idol, weil ich sehr unterschiedliche Interessen entwickelte. Einerseits interessierte mich Sinan, der osmanische Baumeister des 15. Jahrhunderts, wie er die Kuppelräume ausweitete und wie er in seinen Moscheen das Licht manipulierte. Ich war auch lange Zeit fasziniert von der Renaissance, von der venezianischen Schule, speziell von Sansovino und wie er den Raum in einer formal reduzierten Weise auf sehr ruhige Art artikulierte. Wenn es Richtung Moderne geht, liebe ich die klassizistische Periode von Boullée und Ledoux. In der Moderne selbst sind es Jørn Utzon und der Argentinier Clorindo Testa, die mich beeindrucken, aber auch Buckminster Fuller und die Metabolisten. Auf der anderen Seite faszinieren mich weit mehr noch die Denker, von Goethe bis zu den aktuellen wie Peter Sloterdijk, Wissenschaftler verschiedener Disziplinen, aber auch Modemacher wie Martin Magiela, einer der innovativsten Designer. Ich weite gerne meine Interessensgebiete aus.
Der für mich wichtigste Lehrer war Mohsen Mostafavi, heute Dekan in Harvard. Er arbeitete eng mit Dalibor Vesely zusammen, der seinerseits am tschechischen

**Falk Jaeger** Did any of your teachers have a particularly strong influence on you?
**Ben van Berkel** There was not one particular person, however, various groups influenced different aspects of my work. I never had a hero because I developed a very broad range of interests. On the one hand, I was interested in Sinan, the renowned sixteenth century Ottoman architect, and how he expanded the dome and manipulated the light in his mosques. Then for a long time I was fascinated by the Renaissance, by the Venetian School, particularly by Sansovino and how he unobtrusively articulated his spaces in a formally reduced way. Then when it comes to more modern times, I like the classical period of Boullée and Ledoux. In the modernist period, architects like Jørn Utzon and the Argentinean, Clorindo Testa, impress me, as do Buckminster Fuller and the Metabolists. On the other hand, I'm even more fascinated by thinkers, from Goethe to contemporary philosophers like Peter Sloterdijk, by scientists from different areas of research, and by fashion designers like Martin Margiela, one of the most innovative designers around. I enjoy expanding my fields of interest.
The most important teacher I had was Mohsen Mostafavi, who is now Dean of the Harvard Design School. He worked very closely with Dalibor Vesely, who was interested

Surrealismus in der Architektur interessiert war. Ich studierte auch bei Zaha Hadid, die mich stark beeinflusste, nicht so sehr durch ihre Bauten, aber durch ihre Arbeitsmethoden, ihre Stärke, ihre Unerschrockenheit. Wenn ich mit einer kleinen Zeichnung zu ihr kam, rüffelte sie: „Nicht so mickrig, mach es fünf Meter groß!" Sie lehrte mich, Stärke zu zeigen.

Und kurze Zeit arbeitete ich in den späten achtziger Jahren bei Calatrava, als er aus meiner Sicht seine stärkste Schaffensperiode hatte.

**FJ** Wie kamen Sie zu Ihrem ersten Auftrag?

**BvB** Es handelte sich um die Decke einer Kunstgalerie. Ich arbeitete drei Monate an diesem Auftrag – er wurde nie gebaut. In der Folge konnte ich jedoch eine Ausstellung junger Künstler im Gebäude der Holland-Amerika-Linie gestalten und machte überhaupt viel Innenarchitektur und Ausstellungsdesign.

Das erste große Projekt, die Erasmusbrücke in Rotterdam, war aus einem internationalen Gutachterverfahren der Stadt hervorgegangen. Ich hatte eine seltsame Idee; ich wollte einen Jagdbogen bauen. Die Pylone sollten mit ihrem Winkel einen Bogen bilden. Niemand hielt die Konstruktion für machbar, aber ich hatte gute Ingenieure, die nachwiesen, dass es funktioniert und nicht nur pure Form ist. Als es geprüft war, gewannen wir den Wettbewerb und hatten sechs Jahre mit meist zehn Leuten gut zu tun.

**FJ** Wie würden Sie in wenigen Worten Ihre Entwurfstheorie formulieren?

**BvB** Meine Entwurfstheorie ist ganz klar mit den Entwurfstechniken verbunden. Man kann als Architekt ein gutes Vorstellungsvermögen und ein gutes Raumgefühl haben, aber wenn man nicht wirklich weiß, wie man Entwurfstechniken ständig aktualisiert und in den Prozess einbringt, kann man das Entwerfen nicht instrumentalisieren. Mir verhelfen neue Entwurfstechniken zu neuen Einsichten, wie man neue Räume entwickeln oder gar Raumexperimente durchführen kann.

Ich bin nicht am Prozess interessiert, aber am Experiment, wie wir entwerfen und wie man Entwurfstechniken bereichern kann, um schlichtweg zu besserer Architektur zu kommen – fast wie ein Künstler. Zum Beispiel Andy Warhol, der Lichtensteins Idee, auf Seide zu malen, erweiterte und damit die Geschichte der Malerei fortschrieb. Mir ist es wichtig, die Möglichkeiten der Architektur durch Entwurfstechniken zu erweitern.

**FJ** Wie muss man sich das vorstellen? Etwa beim Entwerfen eines Museums, eines Wohnhauses oder einer Feuerwache?

**BvB** Mich hat immer die Organisation der Architektur interessiert. Deshalb liebe ich Diagramme, ich habe Tausende gesammelt. Sie geben mir eine Vorstellung davon, wie man die Organisation eines Bauwerks wie das Mercedes-Benz Museum entwickeln und neu denken kann. Die Idee ist eigentlich simpel. Man nimmt eine dreifache Möbius-Schleife und legt sie in zwei Spiralen. Das Prinzip ist natürlich nicht revolutionär neu, das gibt es bei Barocktreppen oder im Vatikan. Aber das Prinzip auf Stockwerksebenen anzuwenden, war für mich eine neue Form, ein Museum zu denken. Ich bin also nicht wie die Modernisten Gropius, Mies und van Doesburg am reduktiven Aspekt der Architektur interessiert, sondern an der Entwicklung, der Entwicklung von Diagrammen.

**FJ** Wenn Sie also ein Gebäude entwerfen wollen, suchen Sie zuerst ein Diagramm als Grundform? Und das kann mathematischer oder geometrischer Natur sein?

**BvB** Ja, es kann fast alles sein, aber es sollte wenigstens ein infrastrukturelles Angebot machen, vielleicht wie eine Straßenkarte.

Michel Foucault spricht von einem Panoptikum. Ich finde die Idee interessant, dass die Organisation eines Gebäudes die kulturellen, politischen und sozialen Verhältnisse wie ein Panoptikum abbildet. Für mich ähnelt das Panoptikum einem Diagramm. Ein Diagramm kann wie das Panoptikum die Idee eines endlosen Raumes hervorbringen oder die Vorstellung, dass es in einem Gebäude kein totes Ende gibt.

Diese Entwurfstechniken waren für mich immer mit bestimmten Themen verbunden, wie die mobilen Kräfte, die Kreuzungspunkte oder die Vorstellung, wie wir mit öffentlichen Beziehungen arbeiten können. Wie wir mit einer Art Kaleidoskop Raumeffekte erzeugen können, damit der Raum um uns ist. Ich war nie von Sigfried Giedions Raum-Zeit-Prinzip überzeugt. Er glaubte an die Vorstellung „Du bist die Kamera". Aber du kannst 20 Kameras

in Czech surrealism in architecture. I was also taught by Zaha Hadid, who had a very strong influence on me; not so much through her buildings as through her working methods. She encouraged me to be bold, not to be afraid. When I showed her a small drawing, she would tell me off and say, "Not so small — make it five metres big!" She taught me to be strong.

And for a short time in the late eighties, I worked with Calatrava during what I consider to be his most creative period.

**FJ** How did you get your first commission?

**BvB** It came about because of a ceiling in an art gallery. I worked on that job for three months — and it never was built. However, as a result of this project, I was asked to design an exhibition of young artists in the Holland-America Line building and I also did a lot of interior and exhibition design work.

The first big project I worked on, the Erasmus Bridge in Rotterdam, developed from an

international report commissioned by the city authorities. I had a strange idea — I wanted to build a bridge in the form of a bow used in archery. The idea was that the angle of the pylons would form the shape of a bow. Nobody believed that the construction could work but I had a team of very good engineers, who proved that it would work, and that it was not just a purist shape. We won the competition when that was verified by the city engineers and for six years we had work for a team of usually ten people.

**FJ** How would you briefly describe your design theory?

**BvB** My design theory is clearly connected to design techniques. As an architect, you can have an active imagination and a good feeling for space, but if you do not really know how to constantly update design techniques and use them in the design process, then you cannot instrumentalise design. New design techniques help me to generate new insights on how you can make different spatial combinations or even carry out new types of spatial experiments.

I'm not interested in the process, but rather in experimenting with the way we design and how we can enrich design techniques so we can simply make architecture better, almost like an artist. For instance, like Andy Warhol, who developed Lichtenstein's idea of painting on a silk screen, which furthered the history of painting. It's important for me to use design techniques to expand the scope of architecture.

**FJ** How should one envisage that way of designing? A museum, for example, or an apartment block or a fire station?

**BvB** I've been always interested in the organisation of architecture, which is why I've always been fascinated by diagrams. I've collected thousands of them. They give me ideas on how to develop and rethink the organisation of a building like the Mercedes-Benz Museum in Stuttgart. The idea is actually pretty straightforward. You take a triple Möbius strip and put it in two spirals. Obviously, this is not a revolutionary new concept —it can be found in baroque staircases or at the Vatican. But applying this principle to different levels was a new way for me to think about a museum. So, unlike modernists such as Gropius, Mies and van Doesburg, who were interested in the reductive aspect of architecture, I am interested in taking a diagram and developing it.

**FJ** So before you design a building, you first look for a diagram to use as the basic shape? And this diagram can be mathematical or geometrical?

**BvB** Yes, it can be almost anything but it needs to provide at least some sort of infrastructure, perhaps the way a map does.

Michel Foucault speaks about the panopticon. I'm interested in the idea that the organisation of a building can express cultural, political, and social conditions like a panopticon. In my view, a panopticon is similar to a diagram. Like a panopticon, a diagram can create the idea of endless space or give the impression that there is no dead end in a building.

sein, die Kamera kann hinter dir, über dir, unter dir sein. Ich glaube, wir leben in vielen Zeiten parallel und ich möchte das in Raumexperimenten ausdrücken.

Aber das war früher. Vom Diagramm gingen wir weiter zu den Designmodellen, über die wir noch sprechen sollten. Und zurzeit gehen wir noch einen Schritt weiter, denn wir machen in letzter Zeit viele Pavillons, die ich als eine Art prototypische Designmodelle für später zu bauende Häuser sehe.

**FJ** Wenn man die Einflussfaktoren für die Architektur so global betrachtet, wenn Sie sagen, „ich lebe in mehreren Zeiten, ich schaue nicht nur in eine Richtung wie eine Kamera, sondern in alle Richtungen, ich entwerfe, indem ich mit *deep planning* alle möglichen Faktoren integriere", führt das dann nicht zu einer Art Beliebigkeit? Denn letzten Endes muss man Prioritäten setzen, weil sich doch nicht alles unter einen Entwurf subsumieren lässt. Im Grunde genommen haben Architekten das ja immer so gemacht. Ich sehe gar nicht das wirklich Neue an dieser Haltung, denn Architekten waren immer Generalisten, die mussten schauen, welche Einflüsse es gibt und mussten diese dann zusammenbringen zu einem Entwurf.

**BvB** Das mag richtig sein.

**FJ** Diese Idee der Entwurfstechnik suggeriert ja eigentlich, dass die ganzen Faktoren, die man in den Entwurfsprozess einbringt, sozusagen automatisch zu einer Lösung führen.

**BvB** Der Pavillon für die Biennale in Venedig ist für mich in dieser Hinsicht bedeutsam. Man kann die externen Einflüsse auf die Architektur wie Politik und Wirtschaft aus- und einschalten, wodurch die Architektur selbst plötzlich an Bedeutung gewinnt.

Wichtig ist für mich die Selbstbeschränkung, die viele Architekten beim Entwerfen aufgegeben haben. In Venedig versuchte ich, eine Wand in das Dach und wiederum in eine andere Wand übergehen zu lassen. Dann senkt sie sich wieder zum Boden und der Boden wird neuerlich zur Decke. So kann ein einziges Teil alles leisten.

In der modernen Architektur versuchten wir die Reduktion, um zu ermitteln, wie weit man abstrahieren kann. Heute, glaube ich, sollten wir den Computer und die neuen Techniken nicht nur dazu benutzen, effizientere und intelligentere Gebäude zu planen. Wir können auch die Ästhetik erweitern, aber dazu ist Disziplin nötig, wie ich es in Venedig versucht habe. Denn einerseits reduziert man die Formen, andererseits wird es auf sehr einfache Art komplexer. Man muss das Denken systematisieren, vielleicht wie ein Biologe oder ein Mediziner die Natur sehen, um Naturphänomene in die Architektur einzubringen.

Bei manchen Projekten gingen wir so vor, wie in Graz, wo wir mit einer simplen Box begannen, die am anderen Ende sehr komplex wurde. Dabei interessiert mich der Weg von der Reduktion zur Komplexität.

**FJ** Würde man heute Architektur eher als biologisches Artefakt verstehen, während man früher, etwa bei Le Corbusier, von einer Wohnmaschine gesprochen hat? Ist die Analogie des heutigen Hauses eher eine biologische?

**BvB** Ich mag das Wort Maschine. Der Computer ist jedoch ein anpassungsfähiges System, komplexer, intelligenter, anders als die früheren industriellen Maschinen. Vielleicht nennen wir ihn biologische Maschine. Das interessiert mich mehr, denn ich hoffe, in Zukunft wird Architektur atmen und mehr lebender Organismus sein.

**FJ** Der Kollege der *ZEIT* hat vom „Barock aus dem Rechner" gesprochen. Welches Verhältnis hat denn Architektur zur szenischen Präsentation? Ist das ein Ziel für Ihre Architektur? Das Bauen von theatralischen Situationen mit dramaturgischem Denken dahinter?

**BvB** Am Barock interessiert mich der klassische Aspekt, nicht der dekorative. Er beschreibt oft sehr klar einen Eingang, ein Treppenhaus. Oscar Niemeyer ist kein Barockarchitekt, aber auch er kann ein Treppenhaus sehr gut gestalten und ihm eine neue expressive Form geben. Es ist Mode, wieder über Dekor in der Architektur zu

In my mind, these design techniques have always been connected to certain topics such as mobile forces, crossing points, or the way we could work with the principles of public constructs. How to generate a kind of kaleidoscopic spatial effect so that we are surrounded by space. I was never convinced by Sigfried Giedion's principle of space and time. He really believed in the idea that, "You are the camera". But you can be twenty cameras. The camera can be behind you, above you, underneath you. I believe that we live simultaneously in many times and this is what I would like to express in experiments with space.

But that was earlier on. From the diagram we moved on to the topic of design models, which we should talk about later. And at the moment, we are even going a step further because we have been designing a lot of pavilions lately, which I consider to be a sort of prototypical design model for future buildings.

**FJ** Looking globally at the factors that influence architecture, when you say that you live in different times, that you don't just look in one direction, like a camera, but in all directions, that you do a deep planning type of design and integrate all sorts of factors — doesn't that lead to a type of arbitrariness? In the final analysis, one has to prioritise because one cannot subsume everything in a design. Basically, this is what architects have always done. I don't see what is really new in that attitude because architects have always been all-rounders, who have had to look at all sorts of influences and bring them together in a design.

**BvB** That may be true.

**FJ** The idea of a design technique actually suggests that all the factors that one includes in the design process automatically bring about a solution, as it were.

**BvB** I believe that the pavilion we designed for the Biennale in Venice is significant in that regard. You can switch the external values affecting architecture, such as politics and commercial values, on and off — and as a result, the architecture itself suddenly becomes very important. I believe that self-restraint is necessary but many architects seem to have abandoned this in their designs. What I tried for the first time in Venice was to make a wall flow into the ceiling and back again into another wall. Then the wall drops down to the floor and the floor becomes the ceiling once again; so one element does everything.

In the modernist era, we experimented with reductionism to see how abstract we could make architecture. What I now believe is that we should not use computers and new techniques merely to plan more efficient and more intelligent buildings. We can also expand aesthetics, but this requires discipline, which is what I tried in Venice. On the one hand, you reduce the forms, but on the other, you make them even more complex in a very simple way. You have to systematise your thinking to incorporate natural phenomena into architecture, perhaps in the way biologists or physicians look at nature.

This was the way we worked on some projects, for instance in Graz, where we started with a very simple functional box, which became very complex in the end. I'm interested in the process from the reductive to the more complex.

**FJ** Can one regard architecture these days as more of a biological artefact, while in the past, people such as Le Corbusier referred to a "machine for living"? Is the analogy of today's buildings more biological?

sprechen. Aber ich finde, wir sollten neue Wege finden, Architektonisches zu erklären, zu artikulieren.

**FJ** Aber Sie haben in jüngster Zeit einige dekorative Designs gemacht?

**BvB** Ja, etwas mehr. Ich bin zum Beispiel fasziniert von Gottfried Semper, weil er nicht über Dekoration und das Ornament sprach, sondern erklärte, wie Falten in der Kleidung die Qualität des Raumes steigern. Es geht darum, den Raum zu artikulieren. Zum Beispiel gibt es im Musiktheater Graz keine Dekors, aber man kann trotzdem die Musik sehen.

**FJ** Auf welche Weise kann man Musik sehen?

**BvB** Auf viele Arten, moderne Arten. In der heutigen Art Schönbergs, der viel über Surrealismus und Atonalität erzählte. Man könnte auch sagen, das Möbius-Haus ist auf eine Art dekorativ, wegen der vielen Formen. Aber all die Winkel von sieben, neun und elf Grad kommen aus dem System und wiederholen sich im ganzen Haus. Das ist für mich eine neue Art des Denkens, des Proportionierens, eine andere Form der Ruhe. Leute, die ins Möbius-Haus kommen, finden es sehr ruhig. Es sieht komplex aus, aber es ist ruhig. Es ist wie mit der Musik von Philip Glass oder Eric Satie. Sie ist sehr komplex, atonal, aber sie ist ruhig, sehr ruhig. In diesem Sinn ist auch das Musiktheater Graz sehr komplex, sehr dekorativ, aber auch sehr ruhig.

**FJ** Braucht man für so ein Gebäude, in das Sie so viel hineingelegt haben an Analogien zu Schönberg, Satie, wem auch immer, eine Gebrauchsanweisung? Ist der Schritt von der Idee zur Rezeption durch den Benutzer, den Besucher, nicht zu groß?

**BvB** Gute Frage. Ich erkläre es Ihnen, aber nur Ihnen. Ich möchte es nicht jedermann erklären müssen. Ich möchte geheimnisvoller werden, wie ein Künstler. Wenn die Leute nichts begreifen, möchte ich ihnen nicht immer alle Geheimnisse verraten. Heute hat Architektur viel mit Ikonografie zu tun. Wenn man es den Leuten nicht ins Gesicht schreit, kapieren sie nichts und das Gebäude ist ein schlechtes Gebäude. Aber meiner Meinung nach werden Gebäude immer interessanter, es braucht Zeit, lieber 20 Jahre als zwei Jahre. Ich möchte, dass die Leute wiederkommen, wie sie ein Buch zweimal lesen oder einen Film ein weiteres Mal ansehen. Ich möchte nicht immer gleich alle Antworten geben.

**FJ** Sie verwenden also nicht nur einen Kode für die Semantik eines Gebäudes, sondern Doppel- oder Vielfachkodierung?

**BvB** Auch das Material. Mich interessiert Doppelkodierung sehr. Eine gute Freundin von mir ist Pipilotti Rist und ich bin stark beeinflusst von ihr. Sie malt mit der Kamera und ich liebe das so sehr, dass ich diese Idee auch in der Architektur ausprobiere.

**FJ** Farbe ist sehr bedeutend für den Nutzer, aber sie ist auch ein wenig heikel, denn manche Menschen mögen sie lieben, andere mögen sie verabscheuen. Man kann dabei eigentlich nur verlieren?

**BcB** Als wir das orange Theater in Lelystad mit dem pinkfarbenen Treppenhaus bauten, wunderten sich die Leute doch sehr. Aber wir dachten uns, wenn du schwarz gekleidet bist, siehst du auf einer pinkfarbenen Treppe gut aus (kleiner Scherz!).

Aber ich bin auch an „farblosen" Farben interessiert. Wie das Himmelblau an der Erasmus-Brücke und andere hellblaue Gebäude – manchmal spreche ich gerne von der „blauen Periode". Erinnern Sie sich, dass Ihre Mutter früher blaues Waschpulver in die Maschine gegeben hat? Man mischt dem Weiß etwas Blau bei und es sieht gleich viel weißer aus. Ich entdeckte also, dass Hellblau keine Farbe ist, sondern Licht aufnimmt, wenn weißes Licht da ist, und selbst intensiv weiß wirkt. Wenn der Himmel aber grau ist, wird es dunkelgrau. Hellblau ist also eine sehr anpassungsfähige Farbe und nimmt alle anderen Farben an. Oder blauer Himmel, in Rot reflektiert, gibt Lila. Mich fasziniert das Farbspiel. Das Malen mit Farben, das Malen mit der Kamera, das Malen mit dem Computer. Ich will mit dem Computer nicht nur mathematisch umgehen, ich liebe es, digital zu malen. In diesem Sinn möchte ich mich von den Computer-Architekten meiner Generation distanzieren. Es bekümmert mich ein wenig, dass man mit dem Computer wirklich alles machen, alles bauen kann. Ich bin für eine disziplinierte Erörterung der Frage, welche Botschaften man mit neuen Formen der Organisation des Bauens vermitteln kann.

**BvB** I still like the word "machine". However, the computer is an adaptive system, and it is more complex and more intelligent than earlier industrial machines. Maybe we can now call it the biological machine. This is of greater interest to me because I hope that architecture in the future can really breathe and become more like a living organism.

**FJ** A journalist from *Die Zeit* referred to "baroque from the computer". What is the relationship between architecture and staged presentations? Is this an aim of your architecture? To construct theatrical situations with a dramaturgical background?

**BvB** I'm interested in the classical rather than the decorative aspect of baroque architecture. It often describes an entrance or a staircase very clearly. Oscar Niemeyer is not a baroque architect but he is very good at designing a staircase and giving it a new expressive form. It has become fashionable to talk about decoration in architecture again. But I think that we should find new ways to explain and articulate architecture.

**FJ** But you recently did some decorative designs?

**BvB** Yes, some. For example, I'm fascinated by Gottfried Semper because he didn't speak about decoration and ornamentation but instead explained how creases in clothing can improve the quality of a space. My concern is to articulate space. In the Graz Music Theatre, for instance, there is no decoration, but you can still see music.

**FJ** How can you see music?

**BvB** In many ways, modern ways. In today's manner of Schoenberg, who talked a lot about surrealism and atonality. You could also say that the Möbius House we designed in Het Goi in the Netherlands is decorative in a certain way because of all those shapes. But all the angles of seven, nine and eleven degrees emerge from the system and are repeated throughout the whole house. For me, this is a new way of thinking, of proportioning, another type of calmness. People who visit the Möbius House find it very calm. It looks complex but calm. It is like music by Philip Glass or Erik Satie. Their music is very complex and atonal, but also calm, very calm. In this sense, the Music Theatre in Graz is also very complex, very decorative, but at the same time very calm.

**FJ** Does the visitor need a user manual in buildings in which you have incorporated so many analogies like Schoenberg, Satie, and whomever else? Is the distance between the concept and the reception by the user and the visitor not too far?

**BvB** That's a very good point. I will explain it to you, but only to you. I don't want to explain it to everyone. I want to become more secretive, like an artist. When people don't understand anything, I don't want to have to tell them the secret the whole time. Architecture today has a lot to do with iconography. And if you don't shout it in their faces, people don't understand and then the building is seen as a bad building. But in my opinion, buildings become more and more interesting over time. It takes time, preferably twenty years rather than two. I want people to come back, the way they read a book again, or watch a movie another time. I don't want to provide all the answers straight away.

**FJ** So you don't use a single code for the semantics of a building, but use double or multiple coding instead?

**BvB** Materials as well. I am very interested in double coding. Pipilotti Rist is a good friend of mine and I have been heavily influenced by her. She paints with the camera and I love this so much that I tried out the idea in architecture.

**FJ** Colour is very important for the user of a building but it is also rather risky because some people may love it, while others can't stand it. So is working with colour a lose-lose scenario?

**BvB** When we built the orange theatre with the pink staircase in Lelystad, people were very taken aback. But we thought, if you're dressed in black, you would look good on a pink staircase. (That was a joke.)

But I'm also interested in colours that have no colour in a way. Like the baby blue of the Erasmus Bridge and some other light blue buildings—sometimes I like to call this the "blue period". Do you remember how your mother used to put blue washing powder into the machine? You mix a little blue with the white and it immediately looks much whiter. I discovered that light blue is not actually a colour but that it picks up light when there is

**FJ** Warum haben Sie eigentlich keinen Individualstil entwickelt?

**BvB** Ich selbst frage mich das öfter; Journalisten stellen die Frage selten. Ich möchte Architektur von ihren eigenen stilistischen Erinnerungen befreien. Wenn man das Blob-to-Box-Diagramm nimmt, bei dem man vom gleichwertigen Raster zu einer informelleren komplexen Struktur kommt, und irgendwo zwischen den beiden Polen spielt, befreit man die Architektur von den formalen Referenzen. Ich bin also kein Blob-Architekt und ich bin auch kein Box-Architekt, ich möchte die Architektur von Einschränkungen befreien. Das ist der schwierigste Aspekt in meiner Arbeit.

Wenn man alle zwei, drei Jahre versucht, sich neu zu erfinden, erntet man viel Kritik: Warum gehst du vom Möbius-Prinzip zu brutalistischeren Formen? Oder die Leute verstanden es nicht, als wir von den hellblauen zu farbintensiveren Gebäuden kamen. Ich bin heute bereit, mich von allem, was ich zuvor getan hatte, zu befreien. Architektur muss freier werden. Warum gelingt das in der Kunst? Picasso hatte vielleicht zehn Perioden in seiner Schaffenszeit. Deshalb sehe ich Mies manchmal etwas kritisch. Man kann ihn nicht kritisieren, denn er war ein brillanter Architekt. Aber Le Corbusier war weitaus innovativer – er war ein Künstler-Architekt.

**FJ** Der konstante Faktor in Ihrer Arbeit ist also kein formaler, sondern die Art zu denken?

**BvB** Und das Experiment. Das Wichtigste ist die Idee, die dann zu intonieren ist, wie mit einem Instrument. Wenn du das Instrument nicht beherrschst, wenn du nicht jeden Tag fünf Stunden übst, wirst du kein guter Architekt sein.

white light and then appears to be an intense white itself. But when the sky is grey, light blue becomes dark grey. So light blue is a very adaptive colour that takes on all different colours. When the blue sky is reflected red, it becomes purple. I'm fascinated by experimentation with colours. Painting with colours, painting with the camera, painting with the computer. I don't want to just use the computer in a mathematical way. I also love to paint digitally. In this sense, I want to distance myself from the computer architects of my generation. It worries me a little bit that you can really do everything, build everything with the computer. I am in favour of a disciplined exploration of what types of messages you can convey with new types of building organisation.

**FJ** Why didn't you develop an individual style in your architecture?

**BvB** This is a question I ask myself all the time but not many journalists do. I want to liberate architecture from its own stylistic references. If you take the blob-to-box diagram, where you move from the standardised grids to a more informal complex structure, and play around somewhere between these two poles, then you liberate architecture from formal references. I'm not a blob architect and I'm not a box architect. I want to liberate architecture from constrictions. This is the most difficult aspect of my work. If you try to reinvent yourself every two or three years, you get a lot of criticism. You are asked why you went from the Möbius principle to a more brutalist architecture. Or when we went from all those light blue buildings to more colourful buildings, people didn't understand that. Today I am willing to liberate myself from everything that I did in the past. Architecture should become freer. Why is it possible in art? Picasso had some ten periods in his work! That's why I'm sometimes critical of Mies van der Rohe. You cannot really criticise him because he was a brilliant architect. But Le Corbusier was far more innovative. He was an artist and an architect.

**FJ** So the constant factor in your work is not formal but rather a way of thinking?

**BvB** And experimenting. The most important aspect is the idea — but then you have to use it like an instrument. If you don't know how to use an instrument, if you don't practise it every day for five hours, then you will not become a good architect.